D0696184

Werner Lant....

The New Parrot Handbook

Everything About Purchase, Acclimation, Care,
Diet, Disease, and Behavior of Parrots

With a Special Chapter on Raising Parrots

50 Color Photographs by Outstanding Animal Photographers,
30 Drawings by Fritz W. Köhler, and
35 Maps Indicating Distribution

Advisory Editor:
Matthew M. Vriends, Ph.D.

BARRON'S

First English language edition published in 1986 by Barron's Educational Series, Inc.

The title of the German book is *Das GU Papageienbuch*

All inquiries should be addressed to:
Barron's Educational Series, Inc.
250 Wireless Boulevard
Hauppauge, New York 11788

International Standard Book No. 0-8120-3729-4

Library of Congress Catalog Card No. 86-17289

Library of Congress Cataloging-in-Publication Data

Lantermann, Werner, 1956 –
    The new parrot handbook.

    Translation of: Das GU Papageienbuch.
    Bibliography: p. 141
    Includes index.
    1. Parrots.   I. Vriends, Matthew M., 1937 –
II. Title.
SF473.P3L3613   1986   636.6'865   86-17289
ISBN 0-8120-3729-4

Printed in Hong Kong

25 24 23 22 21 20 19 18 17 16

The color photos on the covers show

Front cover: Blue and gold macaws.
Inside front cover: Yellow-naped Amazon.
Inside back cover: Tame Moluccan cockatoo sitting on its owner's shoulder.
Back cover: Above: Blue and gold macaws; eclectus parrot; yellow-naped Amazon. Center: Blue-fronted Amazon; lesser sulfur-crested cockatoos. Below: African gray parrot; green-winged macaws.

Photo credits

Angemayer: pages 20 (above, right), 119 (above, right; below, left); Gosebruch: page 10; Hammel: page 66 (above, right); Lantermann: pages 9, 19, 101 (below, left), 102 (below, left and right); Maindok: page 66 (below, right); Martin: page 66 (above, left; below, left) and back cover (above, center); Reinhard: pages 20 (below, left and right), 65, 120, and back cover (center, left and right); Scholtz: pages 101 (above, left and right; below, right), 102 (above, left and right); Schweiger: pages 83 and 84; Skogstad: front cover, pages 55, 56 (above, left), and back cover (above, left; below, right); Wagener: page 119 (below, right); Wothe: pages 20 (above, left), 37, 38, 56 (above, right, below), 119 (above, right), inside front cover, inside back cover, and back cover (above, right; below, left).

Born in 1956, **Werner Lantermann** studied biology and Protestant theology and passed his state examinations in 1986. Since 1981 he has been Director of the Private Institute for Research on Parrots in Oberhausen. He specializes in the large parrots of Central and South America and has written numerous articles for scientific publications as well as several books about African and South American parrots.

Important notes

People who suffer from allergies to feathers or feather dust should not keep parrots. If there is any question in your mind, ask your doctor before buying a bird. When handling parrots, one sometimes gets bitten or scratched. Have a doctor treat such wounds promptly. Psittacosis (parrot fever) is not a common disease in parrots (see page 46), but it can give rise to life-threatening conditions in both humans and parrots. That is why you should definitely consult a doctor if you have any symptoms suggesting a cold or the flu (see page 46).

Contents

Preface 5

Considerations Before You Buy 6
Do Parrots Fit Your Way of Life? 6
A Single Bird or a Pair? 7
Keeping Several Parrots 7
Children and Parrots 8
Vacation Care 8

Advice for Buying Parrots 11
Where to Look for Parrots 11
What to Watch for When Buying a Parrot 12
Age of the Bird at Purchase 13

Housing Parrots 14
An Indoor Cage 14
An Indoor Aviary 16
A Bird Room 17
An Indoor-Outdoor Aviary 21
A Climbing Tree Indoors or Outside 23
Lighting and Heating 23
Dishes for Food, Water, and Bathing 24
Temperature 24

Basic Rules of Care 25
The Trip Home 25
Getting Settled 25
Hand-taming a Parrot 27
Flying Free in the Apartment 29
Mimicking—Not Every Parrot Learns to Talk 29
Toys and Entertainment 30
Keeping the Cage or Aviary Clean 31
Catching a Parrot 31
Grooming Required for a Parrot 31
Clipping the Wings 32
List of Dangers 34

Diet 35
The Basic Birdseed Mixture 35
Fruit and Vegetables 36
Sprouted Seeds 39
Animal Proteins 40
Minerals and Vitamins 40
Drinking Water 41

Diseases and How to Keep Parrots Healthy 42
First Signs of Illness and Measures to Take 42
Ectoparasites 43
Endoparasites 43
Inflammation of the Intestines 43
Salmonellosis (Paratyphoid Infection) 44
Coccidiosis 44
Trichomoniasis 44
Crop Inflammation 45
Disorders of the Respiratory System 45
Aspergillosis 45
Parrot Fever (Psittacosis) 46
Avitaminosis-B (Vitamin B Deficiency) 47
Rickets 47
Feather Plucking 47
Egg Binding 48
Names of Body Parts and Plumage (Figure) 49

Raising Parrots 50
Parrots—a Group of Birds Threatened by Extinction 50
The Washington Convention 50
The Aviculturist's Role in Preserving Parrots 51
The Housing of Breeder Birds 52
Sexing Parrots 53
Sexual Maturity and Determining a Bird's Age 58
Buying Breeder Birds 59
Should You Try to Mate Parrots That Are Kept Singly? 61
Matching Pairs 62
The Molting Cycle and How Temperature Affects It 63
The Right Nesting Facilities 64
Supplementary Foods for the Breeding Period 68
The Incubation Period 69
Problems During Incubation 73
The Development and Rearing of the Young 74
Artificial Incubation and Hand-Raising Young Parrots 76
Hybrid Offspring 77
Bird Shows 78

Contents

Parrot Biology 81
The Scientific Classification of Parrots 81
Distinguishing Characteristics of Parrots 81
Sensory Organs and Capacities 81
The Natural Distribution of Parrots 82
The Natural Habitat of Parrots 85
Parrots Living in the Wild 86

The Behavior of Parrots 88
Nonsocial Behavior 88
Social Behavior 91

Popular Parrot Species 95
Parrots of the Pacific Distribution: 95
Cockatoos 95
  Greater Sulfur-Crested Cockatoo 95
  Lesser Sulfur-Crested Cockatoo 96
  Moluccan Cockatoo or Salmon-Crested
    Cockatoo 97
  Umbrella-Crested Cockatoo or White
    Cockatoo 98
  Goffin's Cockatoo 99
  Bare-Eyed Cockatoo or Little Corella 100
  Rose-Breasted Cockatoo or Galah 103
Eclectus Parrot 105
The Parrots of Africa: 106
Long-Winged Parrots 106
  Senegal Parrot 106
  Brown Parrot or Meyer's Parrot 108
  Jardine's Parrot 108
African Gray Parrot 109
Parrots of the South American Distribution: 111
Amazons 111
  Spectacled Amazon or White-Fronted
    Amazon 112
  Green-Cheeked Amazon or Mexican Red-
    Headed Amazon 113
  Finsch's Amazon 114
  Yellow-Cheeked Amazon 114
  Blue-Fronted Amazon 115
  Yellow-Fronted Amazon or Yellow-Crowned
    Amazon 117
  Orange-Winged Amazon 118
  Mealy Amazon 121

Parrots of the *Pionus* Genus 122
  Red-Vented Parrot or Blue-Headed Parrot 123
  Maximilian's Parrot or Scaly-Headed Parrot 124
  Bronze-Winged Parrot 125
Macaws 126
  Blue and Gold Macaw 126
  Great Green Macaw 127
  Military Macaw 128
  Scarlet Macaw 129
  Green-Winged Macaw 130
  Yellow-Naped Macaw 131
  Severe Macaw 132
  Illiger's Macaw 133
  Noble Macaw or Red-Shouldered Macaw 134
  Hyacinth Macaw 135
Caiques 135
  Black-Headed Caique 136
  White-Bellied Caique 137

Endangered and Extinct Species 138
  Parrot Species in Danger of Extinction 138
  Extinct Species 138

**Special Rules for Bringing Pet Birds into the
    United States** 139
  What Is a Pet Bird? 139
  Importing a Pet Bird 139
  Ports of Entry for Personally Owned Pet Birds 139
  The Quarantine Period 139
  Special Exceptions 140
  Other U.S. Agencies Involved with Bird
    Imports 140
  Two Serious Threats to Birds 140

Useful Addresses and Literature 141
  Books 141
  Periodicals 141
  American Bird Clubs 141
  Australian Bird Clubs 141
  Canadian Bird Clubs 141
  English Bird Clubs 141
  New Zealand Bird Club 141
  Veterinarian Association 141

Index 142

Preface

People began to keep parrots in their homes over two thousand years ago. The reason for this popularity was the same then as it is now: These birds delight because of their pleasant nature, their generally bright and colorful plumage, and their talent for imitating the human voice. These qualities are found primarily in the larger species, like the gray parrot, the African *Poicephalus* parrots (e.g., the Senegal, *P. senegalus*), and the Amazons, macaws, and cockatoos. It is these parrots that are often referred to as the "large parrots," regardless of scientific classification, and that form the subject of this book.

The enthusiasm these lovely and intelligent birds evoke in their beholders often leads to thoughtless, spur-of-the-moment purchases. Some people buy a parrot without first finding out what kind of care and conditions their new pet requires. It never occurs to them that they are about to become responsible for the well-being of a bird with very specific demands and that this responsibility may not go away for many years. Parrots living under the care of humans can grow very old. The consequences of improper treatment are likely to be serious, and the parrot owner's disappointment will be great if the bird remains shy, acquires the habit of screeching, or takes to feather plucking.

Werner Lantermann, who has had and bred parrots for many years, offers advice in this book for the proper care of parrots. He discusses acclimation, proper housing, daily living with parrots, and the right food for them. With the help of this information even the beginning parrot owner can learn to take care of large parrots in such a way that they stay healthy for years, that birds kept singly become friendly and may learn to "talk," and that parrots kept for breeding actually do so and raise their young successfully. Accounts of the most important patterns of behavior will help the parrot fancier better understand what large parrots need to be happy.

For centuries almost all the parrots found in cages and aviaries were imported, but in the last few decades some populations of wild parrots have shrunk so drastically that many species face extinction (see page 50). Imports of these birds have therefore been cut back significantly — in accordance with the Washington convention (see page 50) — and have been outlawed altogether for some species. Because of this it is more important today than ever before that aviculturists and fanciers try to get offspring from their parrots. This is why the pet owner's manual includes such a large selection on breeding, a section filled with advice based on actual practice and covering all important aspects of the subject.

Another part of this book that will be of special interest to anyone owning or contemplating ownership of a parrot is the descriptions of different species, where thirty-five more or less commonly available large parrots are introduced. For each of these parrots exact information is given on the special conditions for maintenance, on peculiarities in behavior, and on requirements for breeding. A clear map indicating distribution is included.

The author and the publisher would like to thank everyone who collaborated on this book: the photographers for their excellent pictures, the illustrator Fritz W. Köhler for his informative drawings, and the veterinarian Dr. Gabriele Wiesner for her professional advice in preparing the chapter, Diseases and How to Keep Parrots Healthy.

Considerations Before You Buy

Do Parrots Fit Your Way of Life?

Before you set out to acquire a parrot, let alone several, you should be fully aware that this step means a long-term commitment. Parrots need special care and conditions. If you want to enjoy your bird or birds in the years to come, you have to take time for them and treat them with consistent patience. So, before you make any purchase, review whether you are willing and able to put up with the inconveniences listed below, that are associated with owning a parrot.
• Parrots are messy. Leftover food, bird sand that has been kicked out of the cage, and bits of old feathers have to be swept up in the cage area at least once a day. In addition, feather dust produced in significant amounts by most parrot species (especially by cockatoos) necessitates frequent cleaning of the entire apartment.
• Parrots have to have fresh water, bird food, and fruit or other treats every day. Cages and aviaries require cleaning once a week, disinfecting at regular intervals, and periodic replacement of perches and climbing branches (see page 31).
• Your birds will need good, reliable care when you go on vacation or if you should get sick (see page 8).
• Parrots that are kept in cages have to be given a chance to fly free for at least a couple of hours a day. Or, if their wings are clipped, they have to be allowed to move about outside their cage or on a climbing tree. At these times supervision is essential because flying birds like to alight on furniture and nibble at it. They also land on lamps and may chew on electric wires (with potentially fatal consequences). But even "grounded" birds like to go exploring and can get into mischief.
• Parrots that are kept singly need consistent contact with their owners, who become their surrogate partners (see page 7). If a single bird is frequently left alone for hours or for the entire day, it may develop a neurotic compulsion for screaming or feather plucking.

This spectacled Amazon is holding a peanut with its toes. Most large parrots use their feet to pick up and hold on to large pieces of food.

• Most parrots have a habit of screeching loudly several times a day, especially early in the morning and at dusk. If you have close, noise-sensitive neighbors, ask yourself whether you can reasonably expect them to put up with these "jungle sounds." Ask your neighbors — before you bring home a parrot — how they feel about having a loud-voiced

6

parrot next-door. Many parrot owners have had to get rid of their pets because of their neighbors' protests.

• Combining parrots with other pets in one household can be problematic. Large parrots should never be in direct contact with smaller birds, including smaller members of their own family, like budgerigars (or parakeets), because a confrontation may be fatal for the physically weaker bird. Coexistence with cats and dogs is generally peaceful once the different "parties" have had a chance to get used to each other under your supervision.

• Parrot owners intent on raising young parrots should be aware that getting several birds of the same species does not guarantee offspring (see page 59). Even if breeding efforts are successful, they are not likely to pay off financially in spite of the fact that some parrot species command high prices. Anyone who looks on parrots as an investment and speculates on quick returns through selling young parrots should shift his or her interests to more promising ventures.

Important reminder for beginners: Never buy a parrot impulsively. First find out all you can about the conditions and care the species that appeals to you requires (see Descriptions of Parrots, page 95).

A Single Bird or a Pair?

Large parrots, especially Amazons and gray parrots, are often kept singly. People buying their first parrot generally want a tame bird and preferably one that talks. They usually buy a single bird, keep it in an indoor cage, and go out of their way to hand-tame it and teach it to talk.

A single tame bird that seems to have accepted its owner as a surrogate partner can be a source of great pleasure. No matter how enjoyable the partnership may be from the human standpoint, however, it is only a makeshift solution for the bird. Most parrots are sociable, gregarious creatures that need contact with members of their species. A parrot that has overcome all fear of humans and lets its head be scratched by its caretaker or even engages in courtship displays does so only because there is no true partner around. Programmed by nature to need social contact, it will ultimately make do with whatever is available, in this case a human surrogate. But I strongly urge you, if your finances and your living space permit, to buy a second parrot, preferably of the same species. I say this even though two birds are more interested in each other than in their caretaker and may not become as tame. Parrots of different species sometimes also accept each other as partners.

Keeping Several Parrots

If you have more than two parrots you will probably not want to keep them in your living room but will house them instead in a separate bird room (see page 17) or in an outdoor aviary with attached shelter (see page 21). Chances are that if you have several birds your motives for keeping parrots will have changed, too. Sooner or later you will want to try to breed them. You will want to make an effort to help preserve parrots, some of which are threatened with extinction, because you have begun to care deeply for these gorgeous tropical birds and feel responsible for their fate.

Children and Parrots

Large parrots can represent a real danger for babies and very young children. When there is a new baby in the family, a parrot that has been the center of attention up to now can create scenes of jealousy and bite the baby. This is no reason to give the bird away, however. If you take care not to neglect the parrot, it will in time get used to the new family member. Still, you should make it an absolute rule never to leave a baby alone in the same room with a large, uncaged parrot. The same goes for young children. A parrot may inflict painful wounds on a small child because the child doesn't anticipate the sudden jabs of the parrot's bill and therefore can't get out of the way quickly enough.

School-age children usually have no problem getting along with a large parrot. They quickly get to know the bird's habits and peculiarities, and it doesn't take them long to learn to read its moods.

Vacation Care

You have to plan ahead in good time to find a caretaker or a place for your parrot to stay when you go away on vacation or have to be away from home for some other reason.

One possibility is to take your parrot to a veterinarian or pet store that will board animals for a fee (usually for a couple of dollars a day). For the bird it is better, of course, if it can stay in its accustomed surroundings and be fed there twice a day. The substitute caretaker should spend some time each day playing and talking with the parrot so that the bird, which has come to depend on humans for social contact, will not languish in loneliness and boredom. Birds that are kept singly often respond to the absence of their familiar keeper with nonstop screaming or with feather plucking. By contrast, two birds that have been kept together usually accept such a change quite calmly.

Lesser sulfur-crested cockatoo. Of all the cockatoos, the lesser sulfur-crested is the easiest to breed.

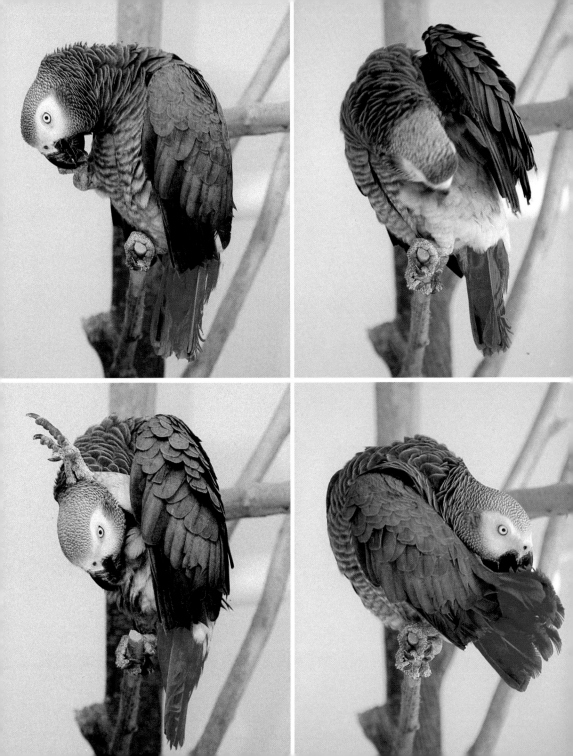

Advice for Buying Parrots

Where to Look for Parrots

Parrots can be purchased from pet dealers and shops, at the pet section of major department stores, directly from importers and quarantine stations, or from private owners.

The parrots most commonly found at pet stores are Amazons, gray parrots, and Senegal parrots; in larger establishments you may also find macaws and cockatoos. If you don't see what you are looking for at a store, you should ask the dealer if the species you are interested in can be obtained. A larger selection of birds will be available from an importer who supplies birds primarily to the retailers, that is, to pet stores. An importer obtains the parrots from the countries of origin and arranges for the officially prescribed quarantine procedures before the birds are offered for sale. Some of these importers occasionally sell birds to private fanciers, although they usually charge higher prices than a retailer. The major import stations almost always have several kinds of macaws, cockatoos, and Amazons, as well as some African grays and Senegal parrots.

Important: Parrot enthusiasts without experience in acclimating parrots (see page 25) should never buy birds directly from an importer. Even though parrots acquired from an import station have undergone an acclimating period of at least 30 days, the risk of sickness or even death is much greater for these birds than for parrots that have spent an additional few weeks in a cage in a pet store after the quarantine period.

◄ Gray parrot preening itself. By twisting and bending, the bird reaches all parts of the body easily — except the head, neck, and throat.

Parrots Sold by Private Owners

Avicultural publications (see Useful Literature and Addresses, page 141) often carry advertisements for parrots for sale by private persons.

Sometimes the advertisement will state that the bird has to be picked up from the owner. In other cases, the owner will offer to send you the bird by mail when you call to arrange for the purchase. Even if you have to travel several hundred miles to pick up the bird, you should never buy a parrot over the telephone and have it shipped. Unlike professional pet dealers, private sellers rarely guarantee that the bird will be alive upon arrival. If you do have complaints about the bird's condition upon its arrival, a telephone call is not likely to produce much satisfaction. It is a rare seller who will take the bird back and refund your money. Nor should you forget the stress and trauma a bird suffers in being shipped through the mail.

I strongly urge you to pick up your parrot yourself and subject it to a thorough examination (as described on page 12).

Parrots Reared in Captivity

Parrots reared in captivity rarely come up for sale, and you will probably have to pursue several routes in trying to obtain such a bird.

• Since pet stores do occasionally carry parrots reared in captivity, you should inquire if and when the kind you are interested in may be available. Leave your address so the dealer can contact you if such a bird can be located for you.

• Look around yourself for experienced and successful aviculturists; addresses are available from breeders' associations (see Useful

Advice for Buying Parrots

Literature and Addresses, page 141). Don't be surprised if the breeder is not able to fulfill your wishes right away. Count yourself lucky if the breeder promises to reserve a bird from the next brood or an even later one.

• Every so often, domestically bred parrots are advertised in avicultural publications (see page 141). You'll probably have to read the classified section over a period of time before you find the parrot you're looking for.

As you can see, buying a parrot reared in captivity takes time and patience. And like other rare objects, these birds command high prices. Since importing large parrots is getting more and more difficult (see page 50), we can only hope that in the future more of them will be bred by aviculturists.

What to Watch for When Buying a Parrot

No matter where you buy your parrot, you should be able to judge the bird's state of health.

Note your first overall impression of the cage, aviary, or sales room when you visit the establishment where you intend to buy your parrot. Pay special attention to the cleanliness of the bird's housing, and check if the bird has the right kinds of food. Before you go up to the bird, watch it for a while from a distance.

A parrot that does nothing but sit in its cage with puffed up feathers, that shows no interest in moving to the outdoor part of an aviary during the day, or that remains immobile with head turned back and eyes closed while the rest of the birds move about vigorously may be sick. If the salesperson

then goes up to the parrot, speaking loudly or gesticulating, he or she may well be aware of the bird's condition and may be trying to startle it into flattening its feathers and thus look sleek and healthy for the benefit of the potential buyer.

When you get closer to the bird, watch for the following.

Plumage: The plumage of a healthy parrot is smooth, glossy, and uninterrupted.

Jardine's parrot with a crossed bill. Malformations of the bill are often the result of wrong diet or improper conditions. Someone just starting out with parrots should not buy a parrot with a misshapen bill.

Freshly imported parrots may look somewhat battered as a result of capture, shipping, and crowded conditions at the quarantine station. This is nothing to worry about if the bird seems healthy otherwise. But if, according to the salesperson, the bird has lived in captivity for several years, you should take a closer look at the plumage. Missing feathers and bald or bloody spots (especially on the breast, the abdomen, and the back) often indicate feather plucking. Birds suffering from this disorder — the causes of which

Advice for Buying Parrots

are not fully understood — bite or pluck out the contour feathers on their bodies. This habit is extremely difficult to break, and neophyte bird owners should avoid buying a bird that shows signs of feather plucking.

Droppings: The droppings of healthy birds are partly olive green and partly white and are firm. Mushy, watery, or discolored droppings may signal sickness. You should be aware, though, that stressful experiences, such as being caught in the aviary, can cause similar changes, but the droppings soon return to normal. Dirty feathers around the vent may also indicate some disorder of the digestive system.

State of nourishment: If you have a chance to catch and inspect the bird yourself, you can check how well nourished it is by feeling the breast. In a well-nourished bird the breastbone can be felt under the muscle tissue. If it sticks out prominently, this could indicate acute emaciation caused by an infestation of endoparasites or by some other illness.

Psychic disturbances: Psychic abnormalities are not uncommon in parrots, but unfortunately they are difficult to detect and evaluate in the brief contact prior to a sale. Be wary of birds that are very restless, seem excessively nervous, or exhibit compulsive movements. If you are offered a parrot that has been kept singly, ask the owner in some detail why he or she doesn't want to keep the bird. It might be a "screecher," that is, a psychically maladjusted animal.

Other signs that should give you pause are clogged nostrils; frequent sneezing (see Disorders of the Respiratory System, page 45); persistent scratching (see Endoparasites,

page 43); abnormal wing and leg postures; missing claws, toes, or parts of toes; external inflammations (such as oozing wounds); and abnormal positions of the upper or lower mandible that keep the bill from closing properly and thus interfere with eating.

Important reminder: If you consider breeding parrots, you should think twice before buying a tame, affectionate bird that has obviously established a close bond with its owner. Often these parrots are so fixated on humans and rely so much on contact with them that they may be unable to readjust and form normal bonds with members of their own species (see page 61).

Age of the Bird at Purchase

There is no way of telling the exact age of an imported parrot, although the legs of immature Amazons and other large parrots are smooth up to 2 years; beyond that time they become scaly, rough, and calloused (for more signs of age, see Sexual Maturity and Determining a Bird's Age, page 58). Shipments of parrots arriving at quarantine stations usually contain birds of all ages, though young birds predominate. The exact age of a bird bred in captivity, however, can be ascertained because a dedicated breeder enters the birth date along with the band number in the breeding record. Obviously, young parrots are easiest to tame, and they also adjust to life in a cage or aviary more readily than fully grown birds that have spent years or sometimes decades living in the wild. (For more signs of age, see Sexual Maturity and Determining a Bird's Age, page 58).

Housing Parrots

An Indoor Cage

Pet stores and pet sections of large department stores sell parrot cages in various sizes
and price ranges. Large models that a pet
dealer does not have in stock because they
take up too much room can be ordered from
manufacturers' catalogs.

The commonly available parrot cages that
are 2 feet long, 2 feet wide, and 3 feet tall
($61 \times 61 \times 91.5$ cm) are inadequate for keeping a single parrot indoors. These dimensions barely suffice for small African
Poicephalus parrots, like the Senegal and the
Meyer's parrots. For medium-sized parrots
(overall length 12–14 inches; 30–35 cm) —
Amazons, small cockatoos, and gray parrots,
for instance — such a cage is too small to
serve as permanent quarters. There is not
enough room for climbing, a form of exercise every parrot needs to thrive. A medium-
sized parrot that is housed in such a cage
should be able to spend all day on a climbing
tree or free in the room so that the cage is
used only for sleeping and eating. Most parrots spend much of the day confined to their
cages, particularly once their owners dis-
cover that the birds leave the climbing tree
and exercise their sharp bills on wooden and
upholstered furniture, on carpets, and even on
electric cords when left alone for long periods
of time. I strongly recommend that you invest
in a larger cage at the very start. The pet
trade offers quite a variety of models
(described as parrot aviaries) that are large
enough to satisfy a parrot's urge for climbing
during hours of confinement to the cage. I
have in mind cages measuring $2 \times 3 \times 4$ feet
($61 \times 91.5 \times 122$ cm) or, for macaws, $2 \times 4 \times 4$
feet ($61 \times 122 \times 122$ cm).

What to Look for When Buying a Cage

Round cages or those featuring turrets, fussy
design, or fancy ornamentation — all of which
interfere with the freedom of movement of
the future occupant — should be avoided.

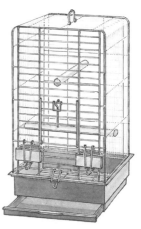

A parrot cage measuring $18 \times 18 \times 30$ inches
($45 \times 45 \times 75$ cm) with a bottom tray that pulls out. A
parrot living in this size of cage has to have a climbing
tree or some other perch outside the cage.

Grating: A cage suitable for parrots has
more horizontal than vertical bars to facilitate
climbing up and down. Otherwise the bird
tries desperately to cling to the vertical bars
but keeps sliding down. The bars should
be about ⅛ inch (2.5–3 mm) thick and be
spaced 1 inch (25 mm) apart.

Many cages have a layer of coarse wire
grating above the floor. The function of this
grate is to keep the bird away from droppings and from spilled food that may be
spoiled. The benefits of this arrangement are
debatable because the grate also prevents

Housing Parrots

the parrot from picking up grit (see page 40), which performs a vital function in digestion and which the bird would otherwise pick out of the litter. A grate at the bottom is useful mostly for newly imported parrots, which sometimes carry parasites, and for sick birds, which should avoid contact with droppings (possibly containing parasite eggs) and leftover food (see Diseases and How to Keep Parrots Healthy, page 42). If you do use the grate, be sure to supply grit in a separate dish.

Bottom tray: A bottom tray that has a separate, removable sand drawer makes it much easier to keep the cage clean. It saves you having to lift the cage, which may be quite heavy, every time you change the sand.

Cage door: The door should be large enough for the bird to get through without feeling frightened, and later, when it is tame, to be moved in and out of the cage on the caretaker's hand.

Accessories for the Cage

Perches: For medium-sized parrots, the perches should be of wood, should be ¾–1 inch (20–25 mm) thick, and should be either round or square with rounded edges. The rule of thumb for all parrots is that the perches be thick enough to allow the bird's toes to reach about two-thirds of the way around. The toenails should not form a full circle and touch. Natural branches — such hardwoods as beech, oak, or ash — make good perches. They should be thoroughly scrubbed with a brush and hot water before being placed in the cage. Branches and perches of softer wood (willow, basswood, or poplar) have to be replaced frequently but should be supplied occasionally because

they satisfy the parrots' need to gnaw and help prevent overgrowth of the bill. The flimsy plastic perches that are often part of a cage's standard accessories belong in the trash.

Food dishes: Most commercially available cages come equipped with just two food dishes, which may lead the new parrot owner to assume that bird food and water are all a large parrot needs. This is far from correct. Parrots need a varied diet (see Diet, page 35) in which the basic mixture is supplemented by sprouted seed, fruit, greens, grit, and calcium. Since each kind of food has to be offered separately, you should have at least four dishes: the two basic dishes for

Food dishes with practical clamps for mounting on the cage or aviary grating.

seeds and water, a third that always holds sand, grit, and calcium, and a fourth in which fruit, greens, and sprouted seeds are alternately offered. If there are baby birds to be raised (see page 74) you may need a fifth dish for egg or rearing food.

All water and food containers should be mounted on the cage walls or placed on the bottom far from perches and thus out of danger of contamination through droppings. Pet stores sell food and water containers with special clamps for attaching to the cage bars (see illustration on page 24) and also dishes made of heavy porcelain or stoneware for placing on the cage floor. The food dishes that come with the cage are usually made of a hard plastic that withstands a parrot's bill quite well. After some use the plastic begins to wear, however, and it gets difficult to keep it completely clean, particularly along the edges. You should therefore replace these dishes every 1 or 2 years.

Litter: You can use commercial bird sand as litter. This sand contains some anise, which acts as a deodorant and keeps your home relatively odor free.

Objects to occupy the parrot: To keep your parrot from getting bored, you should give it some objects to play with, such as a rustproof chain made up of large links, an end of thick rope, a piece of wood firmly attached to a chain, or a wooden toy designed for parrots (available at pet stores). Choose one of these items or, better yet, get several and give your parrot one at the time, replacing it with another when the novelty wears off.

An Indoor Aviary

Pet stores sell indoor aviaries measuring as little as 40 × 28 × 72 inches (100 × 70 × 180 cm) (see illustration on this page). Properly speaking, these are not aviaries at all — an aviary is supposed to offer space for flying — but simply large cages. For most large parrots, except the large South American macaws and the greater sulfur-crested, the umbrella-crested, and the Moluccan cockatoo — these aviaries provide adequate quarters. They could also be used for a pair of

smaller parrots if the birds are allowed out of the cage regularly.

One drawback of these small, commercially available aviaries is that they are quite expensive. Also, many parrot owners want to provide their bird or birds with an environ-

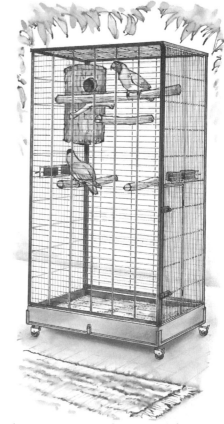

Indoor aviary measuring 40 × 28 × 72 inches (100 × 70 × 180 cm), which could accommodate two small parrots (like the Senegal parrots shown here) or two medium-sized parrots (up to about 14 inches long) if they are permitted regular free-flying sessions.

Housing Parrots

ment that offers more freedom. Building an indoor aviary is not too difficult, and someone handy with tools may well decide to build an aviary of more ideal dimensions.

The first step is to draw up accurate plans to scale. Be sure not to forget the door. A simple aviary can be constructed of spot-welded, galvanized, ornamental grating, available at hardware stores. This grating comes in standard sheets of 84 × 200 inches (210 × 500 cm) with 2- by 2-inch (50 × 50 mm) mesh and a wire thickness of ³⁄₁₆–¼ inch (4–5 mm). If you know the exact measurements you need, you can ask to have the pieces cut to size at the store for a small charge. You can also buy an entire sheet of grating and cut the desired shapes yourself with bolt cutters. When you cut your pieces, make sure that the mesh along the edges is whole because otherwise there is no way to attach the pieces to each other. The ends of the cut wire are very sharp and have to be filed down.

Because this kind of grating is so solid, no frame is necessary for aviaries up to about 6½ × 6½ × 6½ feet (2 × 2 × 2 m). The sections are simply held together with metal clips (from a hardware store) or tied together with strong wire. Metal clips can also be used for holding the door, or you can hang it on light hinges that are welded to the grating. Depending on the height of the door, you will need one or two padlocks to lock it securely. When you are all done, paint the entire aviary with a nontoxic lacquer.

You can build a clean-out tray of plywood or a sheet of metal.

Reminder: For African *Poicephala* parrots this type of home-built aviary is not rec-

ommended because these relatively small birds quickly learn to slip through 2-inch holes.

Accessories for an Indoor Aviary

An aviary is equipped with perches, just like a cage. Depending on their proportions and method of construction, some indoor aviaries allow for short-distance flying. If that is the case, the perches should be located as far apart as possible to encourage the birds to use their wings. Such toys as ropes, pieces of wood, or chains should not obstruct the flight route. Water and food containers (see page 24) can be attached to the aviary walls or set on the floor or on a homemade feeding station. Use a hardwood board for this station or some of the grating left from building the aviary.

A Bird Room

The ideal way to house two or more parrots indoors is to give them a room of their own. You can set the birds up in any unused room or in a bright cellar room that can be heated. A room with a floor area of 9 × 12 or 12 × 12 feet (3 × 4 or 4 × 4 m) would make an ideal home for a pair of large macaws or Moluccan or umbrella-crested cockatoos. If you have more than one pair of parrots of the same or of different species, you should subdivide the room and thus convert it into an aviary room.

Preparations for Setting up a Bird Room

There is some work to be done before you can turn over a room to birds or set it up into separate aviaries.

• Any wallpaper or wall and ceiling coverings have to be completely removed. Then the entire room should be covered with a coat of bright, nontoxic, and preferably washable paint.

• Windows have to be equipped with strong metal screening either inside or out, and all wooden surfaces have to be covered with metal.

• The floor should be easy to clean and have a smooth surface.

• Any electric wires or outlets within reach of the parrots have to be protected with metal pipes or covers.

• If the aviaries to be set up in the room are not self-contained, any radiators that may be present must be covered and the door, which is probably made of wood, has to be replaced with a steel door or replaced with a peck-proof material. If that is not feasible you may be able to construct an antechamber where food and the heater (if movable) can be kept. With this kind of arrangement you will also have to worry less about the birds escaping.

Things to Consider When Setting up an Aviary Room

If you are going to subdivide your bird room into several aviaries, you can either build aviaries of the type described on page 17 or you can subdivide the room itself, using the walls and ceiling for sides, backs, and tops of the aviaries and adding front and subdividing walls made of frames covered with grating. If you choose the latter method, you need considerable building skills to achieve the necessary perfect fit. Getting the wire netting to stay tight when you stretch

it over the frames requires the use of welding tools. For people less manually talented, manufacturers offer prefabricated parts (wall sections as well as cage doors equipped with food racks), but these parts come in only a few standard sizes (for instance, 40 inches wide and 80 inches tall or 20 inches wide and 80 inches tall; 100 × 200 cm and 50 × 200 cm). You can find out more about the construction of aviary walls and doors and about turning a room into an aviary in specialized publications (see Useful Literature and Addresses, page 141). Detailed building instructions would take up too much space here, but I do want to mention two basic rules that you should keep in mind when setting up an aviary room.

• Every aviary (or aviary subdivision) should be about 40 inches (100 cm) wide. The length depends somewhat on how much room you have, but I would recommend a minimum of about 80 inches (200 cm).

• To avoid displays of aggression between different species or between incompatible members of the same species, I would suggest that the subdividing walls be made of a solid material that cannot be seen through (sheet metal or some synthetic material). If you want to use the frame and wire netting construction, use two layers of fine-meshed wire separated by 3 or 4 inches (8–10 cm).

I have seen again and again that when only one layer of wire netting separates the aviaries, neighboring parrots, especially males, engage in fierce fighting through the walls.

A green-winged macaw representing a bad case of feather plucking. Macaws that are kept singly often turn into feather pluckers if their owners don't pay enough attention to them every day.

Housing Parrots

Parrots of the same species are especially ferocious when housed in adjacent aviaries. If you want to have several different species, genera, or tribes — Amazons, gray parrots, and cockatoos, for instance — never house birds of the same kind next to each other with only a single layer of wire netting between them. The same applies to different species of the same genus. At the moment I have fourteen Amazons, seven of them blue-fronted Amazons that I keep in alternate aviaries, with the other species occupying the aviaries between them. This arrangement to a large extent eliminates serious fights through the wires, fights that can leave the weaker party with some toenails or parts of toes missing.

The individual aviaries in a bird room are outfitted just like regular indoor aviaries. Make sure when you mount the perches and set up the climbing tree that the flight paths remain clear.

An Indoor-Outdoor Aviary

If you think you might want to try to raise parrots yourself, you will have to have an outdoor aviary with an attached shelter in order to realize this ambition. Again, space does not permit me to discuss in detail what is involved in building such a structure, and I can only refer you to specialized literature (see Useful Literature and Addresses, page 141). I would like to draw your attention to a few points that you need to take into consid-

eration in the planning and building of a combined indoor-outdoor aviary.

The Enclosed Shelter

In most localities you need an official building permit (generally from a planning board) before you can build an enclosed shelter for your parrots. If it is to be a large structure with a foundation, you may have to submit actual building plans when you apply for the permit. In many towns smaller structures can be erected without a permit as long as they are below a certain size.

If the "town hall" does not approve your plans and you cannot settle on a mutually acceptable compromise, you still have the option of building a shelter without a foundation. For this type of construction you can use regular boards nailed onto two-by-fours. Good insulation is important and can be provided by filling the air space between the inside and outside walls with fiberglass or Styrofoam. If you do use wood for the construction, the inside walls have to be covered with metal or a synthetic material to protect them against damage caused by the parrots' strong bills.

Here are some other features you should consider when you draw up plans for a bird house.
• The shelter should have a power source, some form of heating, and running water, and it should be connected to a sewage system.
• Be sure your birds will have adequate light (see page 23). If lights have to be installed, a licensed electrician should do the job.

Beak shapes of different parrots. Above left: Hyacinth macaw. Above right: Green-winged macaw. Below left: Gray parrot. Below right: Goffin's cockatoo.

Housing Parrots

• I would recommend installing a burglar alarm system, especially if the parrots are at some distance from your home. One reads all too often in avicultural publications of parrot thefts in which the thieves obviously knew what they were looking for. Most of the parrots that are stolen are rare and valuable birds.

The best alarm systems are those that make a loud noise and at the same time activate a bright floodlight, thus both announcing the presence of the thief and scaring the thief away. An alarm that goes off in the owner's house is much less effective because then the owner has to go out into the dark night to try to find the thief, exposing himself or herself to the danger of attack. You can do some things to discourage potential robbers when you build your bird house. Plan to use glass bricks instead of regular glass in the windows, and install a strong door with a safety lock.

An Outdoor Aviary

Outdoor aviaries are always connected to an indoor shelter. The average size of an outdoor aviary for medium-sized to small parrots is about 3 × 10 feet (1 × 3 m), with a height of 6½–8 feet (2–2.5 m). Larger parrots need a flight area about 16 feet (5 m) long.

Aviaries should have a brick or poured concrete foundation or a floor made of large tiles to discourage rats and other undesirable creatures.

For the framework of the structure, I recommend either galvanized pipes or square metal posts. Wood is not desirable partly because parrots gnaw at it and partly because it doesn't hold up nearly as well as metal.

The grade and fineness of the grating depend on the size of the birds and on the strength of their bills. Smaller species, like Senegal parrots, can squeeze through the holes in 2- × 2-inch (50- × 50-mm) grating; greater sulfur-crested and umbrella-crested cockatoos are capable of biting through 1-m wire. (For these birds, ¼-inch bars, 4–5 mm, should be used.) The best system is to have two layers of grating around an outdoor aviary, one made of strong bars on the inside that withstands attacks by parrot bills, and a finer mesh with ½- × ½-inch (12- × 12-mm) holes on the outside to keep out intruders.

A climbing tree you can build yourself. You will need a tub, gravel and sand, a log with holes drilled into it, and three thick branches with several forks.

Housing Parrots

The outer mesh has to be far enough away from the inner layer to be out of bill's reach.

It is advisable to protect part of the outdoor aviary with a roof. Use regular roofing material for this. A hard plastic that lets through light, if used over a sizable area, creates a buildup of heat in the summer and may thus lead to heat stroke.

With most parrots there is no point in planting the aviary because the plants would not survive long under the attack of the parrots' bills.

A Climbing Tree Indoors or Outside

A climbing tree indoors provides a change of scenery as well as more freedom of movement for your parrot. It will quickly learn to fly to the tree from the cage, and if you feed it exclusively in the cage it will return there in the evening of its own accord. Tame parrots often like to get a ride back and forth on their caretaker's hand.

Of course it would be easy to set up a large climbing tree outdoors for the parrot to spend its time during the summer. To forestall a possible escape, however, you would have to put the bird on a chain, which is illegal, or clip its wings. I consider both these measures more cruel than restricting a parrot to an aviary where it can still use its wings as nature intended them to be used and where it is not hampered by a chain. That is why I generally argue against keeping parrots outside without an enclosure, even though I readily admit that in some special cases a climbing tree in the garden may work out well.

Lighting and Heating

Because of their active metabolism, all birds held in captivity should get 12–14 hours of light, preferably daylight, so that they eat enough and, if they are raising young, can feed the nestlings adequately. This means that you will have to provide supplementary lighting in dark rooms and during winter when the days are short. To supplement natural daylight in a bird room or indoor shelter, fluorescent lights, which are energy efficient, are ideal. They are available in various sizes and with different wattages. If you keep your parrot in a room that is also used by the family, you can use a regular incandescent light bulb (75 or 100 watt) in a ceiling fixture.

If you are unable to turn the light on and off reliably at the required hours, you should install a timer that can be programmed to do the job. Since birds need time to retire to their sleeping places, pet stores sell timers with dimmers. These are very practical, although more expensive than simple timers. These combination timer/dimmers can be set to decrease the light in the evening in small increments, taking between 15 minutes and 1 hour to reach total darkness. In the morning the light comes on equally slowly. You can "set" the length of dusk and dawn. If you don't want to invest in this kind of device, you should keep a night-light on when you turn off the main lights to give the birds a chance to find their sleeping places. A night-light is a good idea anyway because it helps the birds stay calm instead of fluttering off in a panic if they are awakened suddenly in the middle of the night.

Housing Parrots

Umbrella-crested cockatoo taking a bath. Glazed earthenware bowls make good bathtubs. They can be placed on the aviary floor or, as shown here, mounted on a special stand.

Dishes for Food, Water, and Bathing

Commercial parrot cages come equipped with standard food and water dishes (see page 15). However, if you keep several parrots in an aviary or bird room you will need larger containers. You can buy practical and large enough dishes at pet stores. Semicircular and round cups made of stainless steel, with rounded edges, are easy to keep clean and very practical. They can be hooked securely to the aviary walls or the food rack, and a safety catch makes it impossible for the parrots to unhook them. If you want to feed the parrots on the floor or at a feeding station, you can buy round, shallow pottery bowls with white glaze on the inside. These dishes also are easy to clean and normally last well. The size and number of dishes of course depends on how many parrots live in the aviary and what kind they are.

A glazed pottery bowl also serves well as a bathtub. It should measure about 14–16 inches (35–40 cm) across and be about 2 inches (4–5 cm) deep. You can simply put it in the bottom of the aviary (not near perches) or on a special metal stand (see illustration on this page). The stand is either rammed firmly into the floor or cemented in so that the parrots can land on the bathtub without making it shake or knocking it over.

Temperature

Parrots living indoors all the time in the same room with people or in a room of their own are usually kept at what we consider a comfortable indoor temperature. As long as the humidity is high enough (60–70%), this temperature will agree with them. You have to be careful not to let the temperature drop too much when you air the room in the winter. Better air briefly several times a day than only once a day, leaving the windows open too long. (Avoid drafts!)

If you keep your parrots in an indoor-outdoor aviary, the temperature in the indoor shelter should not drop below 50°F (10°C) if at all possible. Significant changes in temperature should be avoided, and the heating should be even and reliable. The connection between temperature and reproductive behavior is discussed in the section The Molting Cycle and How Temperature Affects It on page 63.

Basic Rules of Care

The Trip Home

When you buy your parrot you should take it to its new home without delay. The box you transport it in should be bare except for a solidly mounted perch. It should be just large enough for the parrot to fit in comfortably without pushing against the top with its head. The box should never be so large that the bird might be tempted to flutter around in it and hurt itself in the process. If the trip is a fairly lengthy one, food and water

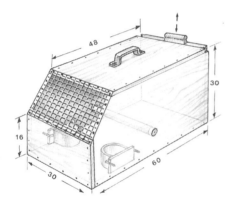

A transport box for a parrot you can build yourself. You will need wood, ⅜–⅝ inch thick, and some fine hardware cloth. The box opens and shuts by means of a sliding door or trapdoor at the back.

(or moist bread) have to be supplied in containers that are placed so that they cannot be knocked over. You can buy transport boxes at pet stores or build one yourself (see illustration on this page). Never transport your parrot in a cage. The bird would flutter around and get hurt.

Getting Settled

Parrots that are purchased from a pet store or from a private source are usually accustomed to living in a cage and to a kind of food you can supply easily (see page 35). For these animals, getting settled means adjusting to the new owner and perhaps to other birds. With parrots that come directly from an import station and have been in the country for only a month, the story is very different. They are still adjusting to different food and a new climate; they have just undergone medical procedures prescribed by law to control diseases (especially to prevent exotic Newcastle disease and psittacosis), and life in a cage or aviary is still foreign to them. They cannot by any means be considered acclimated when they are sold after 4 weeks of quarantine under veterinary supervision. Their natural resistance to disease is lower by the trials they have recently undergone, and they get sick more easily than birds already used to captivity. Never introduce a freshly imported parrot to birds you already have right after bringing it home.

Acclimating Aviary Birds

When your newly purchased parrot arrives, it is best to house it in a smallish cage at first and keep it away from any other birds. It should stay in this cage for 3–4 weeks. This gives you time to observe the newcomer, get to know its peculiarities, watch what it eats (and perhaps introduce some changes in its diet), and slowly win its trust. During this second "quarantine" period, you should have the parrot's droppings analyzed by an avian veterinarian. If anything abnormal shows up, such as parasites at various stages of their life cycle, the veterinarian can recommend the proper medication. After the treatment, a second stool sample should be taken. Only when you have proof that the medication worked should you allow the parrot to leave its confined quarters and move into a community of birds.

Adjustment to an Aviary

When newly purchased parrots are moved into an aviary, its often turns out that they fly only poorly or not at all. Some plummet to the ground like a rock every time they attempt to fly. Generally there is no need to be alarmed, however. Bird catchers and dealers in the parts of the world where parrots come from routinely clip the birds' wings on one side to keep the captured parrots from escaping. Within 1 or 2 years the feather stumps fall out and are replaced by new, perfectly functional flight feathers. If the often brutal treatment of native catchers and dealers has not resulted in permanent damage to the feather-producing tissue, the parrots regain their full capacity for flying.

If you do have a bird that cannot fly properly, you have to watch it closely because it is at an obvious disadvantage compared with fully mobile competitors. By placing extra branches at strategic locations, you can help make all parts of the aviary, especially the feeding stations, accessible to a handicapped bird either "on foot" or by climbing. Still, you should make sure that the bird gets enough to eat and is not crowded out by the other occupants of the aviary.

The acclimation process is not completed until a parrot has slowly and fully adjusted to the temperatures of its new geographic environment and the molting cycle is synchronized with the seasons of the new home (see How Temperature Affects It, and the Molting Cycle page 63).

Adjustment of a Single Bird

When you bring a parrot home, forget any generalizations you may have heard, such as that this kind of parrot learns to talk quickly or is easy to tame or has this or that quality. Instead, approach the bird without any preconceived notions or expectations and simply concentrate on its individual personality.

Every large parrot is intelligent and sensitive and has special traits that you cannot miss if you are observant. Your first and most important job is to watch the animal closely. Its behavior will tell you whether it is healthy, whether it is comfortable, when it is frightened, and when it is hungry. Except for the crucial daily feedings, you should approach the cage as little as possible during the first few weeks. Major cleaning should be postponed until the newcomer has begun to relax in its new surroundings. Avoid abrupt movements, loud noises (such as running a vacuum cleaner), and raised voices. It is well worth treating your new feathered friend with utmost gentleness, talking to it in a soft, soothing voice, and filling its food dishes calmly and unobtrusively so that it will overcome its initial shyness more quickly.

As time goes on, your parrot will let you know when you can stop tiptoeing around it. Each day it gets a little more relaxed in its new environment, and at some point it will stay unruffled even when the telephone or door bell rings, when the blender is on in the kitchen, or when you vacuum its room.

Basic Rules of Care

Almost all large parrots are arch conservatives and regard any innovation with distrust. Strange food, new objects in their field of vision, and unfamiliar or striking clothing worn by the caretaker arouse their suspicion. Parrots unused to changes may be so disturbed by them that they may stop eating temporarily if you put their food dishes down in the wrong order and they don't find the birdseed in its accustomed place.

Of course, if you go on treating your parrot like a bundle of raw nerves for weeks or months, approaching it gingerly and trying to protect if from getting upset or frightened, you may achieve the opposite of what you wanted. The parrot may never overcome its shyness and be so easily frightened that it will flutter off in panicked flight the first time you make an unanticipated move. A parrot has to be confronted gradually with the normal sounds and events of its new environment so that it can learn to deal with them calmly. Birds thus trained to live in the world of people usually realize quickly that they are safe from dangers. After an initial period of orientation, they become trusting — and often quite tame — members of the household. They hardly ever respond with fear to normal events but, on the contrary, take a lively interest in everything that is happening around them.

Hand-taming a Parrot

Before giving some tips on how to hand-tame a parrot, I would like to ask all parrot owners to read and consider the following thoughts.

Anyone who hopes to eventually breed parrots should ask if it makes sense to foster great closeness between bird and human initially and later thrust the bird back into an avian community. It is true that there are many accounts of tame cage birds that did later, after several attempts, raise offspring. I still feel strongly, however, that birds intended for breeding should be introduced directly to others of their own kind without first forming an attachment to humans.

If you hope to turn your parrot into a friendly, hand-tame companion, you have to invest a great deal of time and patience in the effort. Whether you will succeed, no one, not even the greatest parrot expert, can predict. Some parrots quickly accept their keepers and display their trust by letting themselves be picked up and allowing their heads to be scratched. Others keep at a distance as long as they live. They may accept a treat from the keeper's hand or enjoy an occasional scratching of the head with a little stick but will always shy away from any direct touch. These parrots probably associate the human hand with some bad experiences when they were captured or during quarantine.

Tips for Taming a Parrot

The first important point to remember when trying to tame a parrot is to give the bird enough time to adjust to its new surroundings before any training begins. Not until the parrot feels relatively secure in its new home is it time to proceed to the first step of taming, namely, to get it used to your hand. It has to be so familiar with its environment and the various sounds and sights of its environment that nothing in the normal daily routine fazes it. Above all, it has to overcome enough of its initial shyness to realize that you mean it no harm. It also should recognize your voice.

Getting a bird used to the human hand is more difficult when dealing with small, expert flyers, such as the African *Poicephalus* parrots and caiques, than with less agile ones like macaws, Amazons, gray parrots, or cockatoos. Almost any parrot is quick to learn that food arrives by way of the human hand, and sooner or later these intelligent birds will take food direclty from the hand. Begin by holding out the food — preferably something your parrot loves — inside the cage. If the parrot hacks at your hand, don't pull it back abruptly or cry out. Of course this is easier said than done. The calmer you stay, the less reason the bird will have to resort to its bill for defense. Once the parrot realizes that it can safely take a treat from

Greater sulfur-crested cockatoo preening. Parrots clean their plumage thoroughly several times a day. In order to reach the tail feathers they have to swivel the head 180°.

your hand, it is time to go on to the next step, namely, scratching the bird's head through the bars. It is usually not difficult to lure the bird close to the cage wall with some treat it likes. Hold the treat up to it, and try to scratch its head gently while it tries to get the treat.

Things will not go quite as smoothly the first day you try to reach into the cage to scratch the bird. It will retreat, regard you with new suspicion, and perhaps try to bite your hand. It is important not to get impatient and insist at this point. Instead, leave the bird alone for the time being and try again later. Keep trying every day until its resistance begins to give way and it lets you touch it. At some point it will pluck up its courage and get onto your hand, and later it will not hesitate to sit on your shoulder or use various parts of your body in the course of its acrobatic performances.

The Tame Parrot

In time, parrots come to think of themselves as full-fledged members of the family with all the rights but none of the obligations this entails. They also learn to assert their rights. When they feel they are not getting enough attention, many parrots demand their keeper's notice by whistling or producing other sounds, rattling their food dishes, or screeching nonstop. You obviously cannot always give in to a parrot's wishes for admiration and entertainment; still you should not neglect a single bird too much, or else it might become a screamer or start pulling out its feathers (see Toys and Entertainment, page 30).

Basic Rules of Care

Most tame parrots are friendly only toward the people they know well. Even birds that are quite used to life in captivity and have been part of a family for years still regard strangers with great suspicion. When there is an unfamiliar guest in the house, they retreat to the farthest corner of the cage and act with reserve even toward their caretaker. It is impossible to get them to say any of the phrases, whistle any tunes, or mimic other sounds they ordinarily regale you with all day long. This is especially true if you have bragged about your parrot's amazing repertoire and have promised your guests a performance. Don't let the parrot's stubbornness upset you, and don't try to punish it by ignoring it. Parrots seldom oblige by behaving according to our wishes. Punishment in any form is not only pointless but also destroys the trust that has built up between you and the bird.

Flying Free in the Apartment

Large parrots that are confined to small indoor cages soon become obese and phlegmatic if they are not allowed to get out of the cage occasionally to exercise their wings.

As soon as your parrot is hand-tame, you should open the cage door. Many birds let hours elapse before they avail themselves for the first time of this opportunity to taste greater freedom. One of my red-vented parrots that was temporarily restricted to a small cage waited a full 3 days before it dared emerge from it.

When a caged parrot takes to the air again for the first time, the venture usually ends with a crash to the floor, but in time even birds that were confined to a small cage for a long period recover enough flying dexterity to get around all the obstacles a space designed for human living is likely to contain. The favorite landing spot and perch is usually high up in the room on some shelf or on a ceiling lamp. A safer place for landing would be a large climbing tree you can buy at a pet store or build yourself (see illustration on page 22).

You should never leave a parrot alone when it is free in the apartment because it may do considerable harm to furniture and other objects with its strong bill. Also, chewing on electric wires could be fatal to the bird. At first you will have to help your parrot get back to its cage after every free-flying session. If it is tame enough to climb onto your hand or a stick you hold out to it, you can carry it back to its cage easily. Or you may be able to lure it back with a favorite treat. After a few days it will return on its own, especially if it is fed only in the cage.

Mimicking — Not Every Parrot Learns to Talk

People have always been intrigued with birds that "talk" or mimic. The repertoire of talented parrots ranges from imitations of various kinds of sounds to perfect reproductions of words and phrases. Many parrots show no interest in human speech, however, and only learn to whistle a few notes.

If you want a parrot that will talk, make sure you start with a species that has a talent in that direction. Some of the smaller parrots belonging to the genera *Poicephalus* (e.g., the Senegal parrot), *Pionites* (caiques), and *Pionus* (e.g., the blue-headed parrot) can hardly be counted among the talking birds.

Basic Rules of Care

Chances for success are better with any of the other large parrots. The imitations of cockatoos, macaws, and Amazons are generally not as clear and precise as those of gray parrots, which are the acknowledged masters (see page 109).

Not every parrot of a talking species chooses to make use of this talent. Some large parrots never learn to say a single word, and others content themselves with mimicking a few notes or other sounds.

Two conditions have to be met for parrots to learn to talk. First, they have to overcome their natural distrust of humans, and second, they have to be kept singly. Only a parrot deprived of contact with others of its kind will try, in an effort to communicate, to mimic words and other sounds it hears from its surrogate human partner. Parrots that live in pairs or in an aviary community hardly ever make use of their innate ability to copy sounds.

Parrots, like some other birds, are natural mimics. This means that they imitate sounds

Parrots that get along well together preen each other's feathers, especially in the spots they cannot reach with their own bills.

and words they hear over and over again; in other words, you have to repeat what you want them to learn hundreds of times. The best time for these training sessions is in the early evening. That is when the parrot's powers of concentration and absorption are greatest.

In my opinion, stories supposedly demonstrating that parrots use words intelligently (expressing desires, pleasure, or objection) should be relegated to the realm of myth or fable. It is true that some parrots produce words or sounds in appropriate contexts (see African Gray Parrot, page 109).

Toys and Entertainment

Parrots kept singly in a cage as well as birds living in an aviary need toys to occupy them and entertainment to break up the daily routine.

If you cannot afford two parrots, a single bird will in time form a close bond to you, accept you as its surrogate partner, and take up a good portion of your free time. If the bird is to stay happy and content, you have to pay frequent and regular attention to it. It may want to be next to you constantly, sit on your shoulder, and ask to have its head scratched. When you go away on vacation or cannot devote as much time to it as usual, it may react with constant screaming or with feather plucking.

One way to reduce the bird's dependency on you is to let it fly freely inside the house as often as possible and to give it a piece of wood, a large-link chain, an end of thick rope, or anything else suitable for climbing and chewing on. Pairs of birds and birds

Basic Rules of Care

living communally, too, appreciate toys. Although these birds are much less likely to lapse into lethargy, they too are grateful for every shower or new opportunity to play.

Keeping the Cage or Aviary Clean

An important factor in successful aviculture is keeping the birds' quarters clean at all times. Droppings and bits of spoiled food are the breeding ground of many pathogens.

Indoor cages should get a routine cleaning once or twice a week. Remove droppings and leftover food. Replace sand as needed. Scrub dirty perches. Every 2 or 3 months, a more thorough cleaning is in order. Remove the sand tray, empty it, wash it with hot water, and disinfect it. Hose the cage down with hot water in the shower or bathtub, and scrub the perches.

A bird room or aviary should be cleaned with a leaf rake once or twice a week and, if needed, a fresh layer of sand added. Floors made of concrete or tile should have all the sand removed twice a year and be hosed down, scrubbed, and disinfected. Outdoor aviaries built on natural ground have to be spaded twice a year. Turn the earth or replace it with clean soil to a depth of at least 10 inches (25 cm).

Food and water dishes have to be scrubbed clean daily, especially if they are used for soft food, fruit, or sprouts.

But don't go overboard and pick up every bit of fruit or every dropping the moment it hits the ground. Such constant fussing and disruption for the sake of cleanliness are surely more harmful than a moderate amount of dirt that is removed once a week.

This is especially true for birds that live in an aviary community and are more easily upset by humans than pet parrots, and it holds even more for birds that are preparing to mate or are sitting on eggs.

Catching a Parrot

Except for completely tame birds that willingly put up with almost anything their keeper does with them, parrots — whether living in a cage or in an aviary — usually have to be captured by force if medication is to be given or some grooming procedure, like nail clipping or bill trimming, becomes necessary. Since parrots use bill and claws to resist capture, it is wise to wear thick leather gloves when approaching them.

The best time to get hold of a parrot is when it is climbing around on the grating of the aviary. Reach quickly for the bird with your gloved hand, holding the head between thumb and index finger and restraining the wings with the rest of your hand to prevent wild fluttering. To support its feet you can hold out a stick of the right thickness, which it will eagerly clutch with its toes.

Grooming Required for a Parrot

The only grooming a parrot requires is a weekly shower or sprinkling and an occasional trimming of the toenails and the tip of the beak.

The Shower

It is a good idea to give your parrot a shower once or — better yet — twice a week to help keep the plumage clean and elastic and to prevent an accumulation of feather dust.

Basic Rules of Care

Newly imported parrots first have to learn to get used to showers. The best way to administer a shower is with a spray bottle designed for watering plants. Soon the parrot learns to appreciate the bath and spreads its wings and tail feathers wide to expose as much of itself as possible to this "rain" (see The Behavior of Parrots, page 88).

During the summer you can use a hose (with the nozzle set for fine spray) to wet down your parrot, and occasionally you can let it enjoy a warm summer shower outside. In an extensive aviary setup it makes sense to install a sprinkler system that can be turned on to simulate a rain shower in all the aviaries at once.

Plan the showers for the morning or the early afternoon at the latest, so that the plumage has a chance to dry by evening.

In indoor-outdoor aviaries and bird rooms, the parrot's need for bathing can be satisfied by setting up a "bathtub" (see illustration on page 24). The bathwater has to be changed every day.

Trimming Toenails and Bill

With caged birds it sometimes happens that the claws and the tip of the bill (the bill of a parrot never stops growing) don't get enough wear and need trimming. If the parrots have rough perches of different thicknesses and are given plenty of wood to chew on, the need for trimming should be minimal. To trim an overgrown bill or overly long toenails, you need an assistant who either holds the bird or does the trimming. Use toenail clippers to correct the shape of the claws or bill, and smooth any unevenness with a nail file.

When you wield the clippers, be careful not to injure the blood vessels, which extend about two-thirds down into the nails. It is not tragic if you accidentally cut into the quick and there is a little bleeding. Sometimes a capillary grows along with the nail, so have some styptic cotton, silver nitrate, iron subsulfate, or a liquid anticoagulant at hand to deal with this minor mishap. Put the bird back in its cage and leave it undisturbed for a few hours to prevent further blood loss through agitated movement. Usually the bleeding stops quickly and there is no lasting damage.

 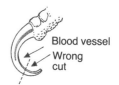

Trimming claws. The drawing on the left shows the right way, the one on the right, the wrong way. Be careful not to cut the part that is supplied with blood. Inside illustration: (left) Proper cut; (right) blood vessel; improper cut.

The bills of parrots hardly ever need reshaping. If a bill does need trimming, be careful, as with the nails, not to cut any blood vessels. It is also crucial that the original shape of the bill, including the tip, be preserved or carefully restored with clippers and file. New parrot owners should ask a pet dealer or a veterinarian to show them how to trim a parrot's nails and bill. If you have any doubt about your ability to perform these tasks, have them done by an expert.

Basic Rules of Care

Clipping wings. Trim the secondaries and the inner primaries (the white part of the feathers) on *both* wings. Never clip just one wing. The parrot would lose its balance when trying to take off, and would tumble to the ground.

Clipping the Wings

Most parrots are shipped to the importers with their wings clipped on either one or both sides. Most parrot owners are glad when new, fully functional feathers replace the old, useless ones and their birds can take to the air again after months of being crippled. But sometimes circumstances require that a parrot's flying be temporarily restricted. This, of course, violates the very nature of birds and is justified, in my opinion, only in very rare cases.

There is one situation in which careful trimming of the tips of the wing feathers on both sides seems justifiable, and that is when a parrot keeps chasing its aviary companions to utter exhaustion. Even here, interfering with nature's way can have regrettable consequences, as one parrot owner told me. He had six blue-fronted Amazons that were housed together in a large aviary. The largest

and most beautiful of them was also the best flyer and ranked at the head of the social hierarchy. Because he bullied his five companions mercilessly, the owner trimmed his wings a little. The bird immediately lost his status and slipped all the way to the fifth slot in the social hierarchy. Upset by this loss of face, he pulled out all his contour feathers, one by one.

Parrots that live outdoors on a climbing tree generally have to have their wings clipped. If this is done properly (see illustration on page 33), the birds are not deprived completely of the use of their wings and can still take to the air, although clumsily, to seek safety from such enemies as cats and dogs. The wings have to be clipped after every molt if the parrot's flying ability is to remain limited.

Clipping just one wing upsets the bird's balance and leads to a temporary inability to fly. Amputation of the lowest joint of the wing cripples a bird permanently. Both these methods are objectionable from the point of view of humanitarian aviculture.

List of Dangers

Source of danger	Effects	How to avoid
Other members of the species (rivals)	Violent fights; growing stress; susceptibility to psychically caused illnesses (see Diseases and How to Keep Parrots Healthy, p. 42)	Be careful in combining birds in aviary communities and watch them closely until a pecking order acceptable for all birds is established
Electric wires	Electric shock from chewing or biting through wires, often fatal	Run wires behind walls, under carpets, or behind furniture, or protect with metal covers; unplug
Poisons	Poisoning from lead, verdigris, rust, nicotine, pans coated with plastic, cleansers, plant pesticides, mercury; also harmful: pencil lead, inserts for ballpoint pens and magic markers, alcohol, coffee, hot spices	Remove all poisonous objects and substances and store out of parrot's reach; don't forget lead weights in drapes; parrots like to nibble on them, so remove them if possible
Poisonous trees and shrubs	Poisoning, often deadly	Avoid giving branches from poisonous trees and bushes, such as acacia, yew, laburnum, viburnum, holly, and all conifers; keep parrots from eating or nibbling on house plants
Windows and glass doors	Bird flies against glass, sustains concussion or broken neck	Hang curtains or teach parrot awareness of the invisible border by lowering blinds two-thirds of the way and raising them a little every day
Large parrots (in an aviary community)	Fights and injuries, in some exceptional cases with fatal consequences.	Never leave parrots of different species together unsupervised
Glues	Death from inhaling evaporating solvents	When using glue (in repairs, crafts, or laying floor coverings) remove all animals from the room and air thoroughly before bringing them back
Kitchen	Steam and cooking odors affect air passages; burns from burners that are turned off but still hot and from hot food in uncovered dishes	Don't keep bird in kitchen: or, if you do, air frequently and briefly — watch out for drafts; put pots of water on unused hot burners; cover pots
Doors	Bird gets caught and crushed if door is opened or shut carelessly; may also escape	Only constant watchfulness can prevent accidents and escape
Drafts	Colds, pneumonia	Avoid drafts at all costs!

Diet

Any food we offer to our captive birds is only a poor substitute for their natural diet. No parrot owner, however hard he or she may try, can match what wild parrots find to eat in their native lands. It is therefore of utmost importance that we do all we can to offer as complete a substitute as possible. The diet we feed our birds has to meet high standards and is adequate only if the following requirements are met.

• The bird's general state of health does not deteriorate in any way.

• The bird's weight remains constant.

• There is no decline in agility or cheerfulness.

• The plumage remains complete and lustrous, and the colors deepen as the bird gets older.

• The birds go through regular mating cycles and successfully raise young.

• No problems turn up, such as killing or plucking nestlings or feather plucking.

Obviously, more than one kind of food is required. Experts, including veterinarians, nutritionists, and veteran bird fanciers, all agree that in the long run deficiency symptoms can be prevented only if the food offered is as varied as possible. The birdseed mixtures and supplements and the feeding rules I discuss in this chapter are based on the long-term experience of many aviculturists. The suggestions that follow will, if observed consistently, help keep your parrots healthy for many years.

The Basic Birdseed Mixture

Except for a few species that have very specialized food habits (species that are not described in this book), all parrots that live in captivity receive the bulk of their food in the form of different seeds. Newly imported birds are introduced to "birdseed" during the legally required quarantine period so that by the time they are ready to be sold they have fairly well adjusted to the common birdseed mixtures. Commercially available birdseed mixtures for parrots are usually composed of the several kinds of seeds that parrots eat. The proportions usually are 60–70% sunflower seeds (white, striped, or black) and about 5% each of peanuts, corn, pumpkin seeds, oats, brown rice, pine tree seeds, and thistle seeds. This kind of mixture is excellent for large parrots, such as macaws, Amazons, eclectus parrots, gray parrots, and cockatoos. For smaller species — brown parrots, Senegal parrots, and caiques — the proportion of small seeds should be increased with silver millet, spray millet, buckwheat, wheat kernels, or canary grass seed (white seed). All these seeds can be purchased separately at pet stores, seed stores, and, in rural areas, at feed stores.

Birdseed should always be available in generous quantities (more than is consumed in 1 day). Many parrots develop a special predilection for certain kinds of seeds and persistently refuse to eat others. It would be pointless to try to force such a bird to eat what it does not like by depriving it of its favorite food. Some parrots would rather starve to death than change their mind about food they have decided — usually for totally impenetrable reasons — is inedible. The greater the variety of seeds and other foods offered, the smaller is the danger that a parrot's strong culinary likes and dislikes will lead to health problems.

Diet

Buying and Storing Birdseed

When you buy birdseed, make sure it is of good quality, dry, and free of dust and parasites. You can easily tell if sunflower seeds, peanuts, or cedar nuts are rancid or moldy by opening the shells. A good way to test the quality of seeds is to sow a few in a shallow dish (see Sprouted Seeds, page 39). If most of them sprout, this indicates high quality. Properly stored seeds remain edible for about 2 years, but the vitamin content diminishes toward the end of the first year. So look for the packing date on the bags, and do not buy seed that was packed more than a year previously. If you buy a birdseed mix or different kinds of seeds in bulk, you have to be careful not only about the length but also the method of storage. Birdseed should be kept in a dry, dark, and airy room. If there is a chance that mice might get into the room where you store the seed, buy a mouse-proof grain bin at an agricultural supply store because these pests not only leave droppings behind but are also disease carriers.

Fruits and Vegetables

Fruit, berries, greens, and other vegetables are an integral part of a balanced diet for parrots.

Fruit: All kinds of parrots need fruit because it is rich in vitamins. Eclectus parrots and some South American species have to have plenty of fruit at all times because in nature they presumably live almost entirely on fruit. Apples, pears, plums, cherries, grapes, strawberries, hawthorn, mulberries, currants, oranges, tangerines, bananas, mangoes, kiwi fruit, and pomegranates are all suitable for parrots.

Greens and other vegetables: Cucumbers, carrots, sweet potato, beets, hydroponic sprouted oats or barley, celery, spinach, tomatoes, lettuce, chicory, Swiss chard, comfrey, and turnip greens can be given to parrots. Fresh corn, especially if it is at the "milky" stage, is popular with parrots and can also be recommended for rearing young birds. Parrots that are not used to fresh corn should at first get only about one-quarter of an ear per day; more may play havoc with their digestive system. Ordinarily, fresh corn is available only in the late summer and in the fall, but you can freeze it in appropriate portions and then thaw what you need for one meal at a time.

Parlsey, which is high in minerals and vitamins, is eaten only reluctantly by most parrots. Beans, brussels sprouts, cauliflower, broccoli, and all kinds of cabbage are bad for parrots and should be avoided.

Wild fruits and plants: Fruits that grow wild (rowan berries, hawthorn fruits, elderberry, and rosehips) are a valuable addition to a parrot's diet. There are many wild plants that can be fed to parrots; a few that are easy to find and recognize are dandelions (leaves), shepherd's purse (leaves and blossoms), chicory (leaves and seeds), and chickweed (leaves, blossoms, and seeds). All parrots appreciate wild plants and fruits, but be sure you know what you are collecting. To mini-

When going after food in their natural habitat, parrots ▶ perform impressive acrobatic feats. Here a yellow-naped Amazon hangs by one foot while eating the fruit of a tree.

mize the risk of picking something harmful, consult a guide to wild plants with descriptions and illustrations of plants that can be fed to birds (see Useful Literature and Addresses, page 141).

Rules for feeding: To prevent possible health hazards, you should obey a few rules when feeding your parrots fruit, vegetables, and greens.

• Buy only unsprayed fruit and vegetables if at all possible. Fruit that is not locally grown is likely to have been harvested some time ago and should be peeled because it was probably treated with some kind of chemical to keep it fresh looking.

• Never gather wild plants and fruits along the roadside because they have probably absorbed poisons from car exhausts.

• Always wash fresh food, whether grown in your garden, bought at the supermarket, or gathered wild, before you feed it to your birds.

• Frozen food — corn on the cob, for instance — must be completely thawed before use.

• Provide as much variety as you can, and don't cut down on something because your parrot (or parrots) only nibbles on it — pieces of fruit, for instance — and leaves the rest. That is part of its natural behavior. Nature is so bountiful that the birds have no need to finish one thing neatly before moving on to the next.

◁ The popular scarlet macaw is an endangered species and may no longer be imported. (It is listed in Appendix I of the Washington Convention.) This photograph shows the bird in its natural habitat hanging head down from a branch.

• Fresh food has to be replaced daily. Wilted, moldy, or rotting food can make a bird very sick.

Sprouted Seeds

In the winter, when greens are not so readily available, and before and during the mating season, sprouted seeds are an important item on the menu of large parrots. Sprouts of indigenous grains, such as oats and wheat, are especially nutritious because they are rich in vitamin B. They can be used at the onset of the mating season to help bring parrots into breeding condition. Parrots also like sprouted sunflower seeds, but these should be given to breeder birds mostly between mating cycles.

Keeping everything clean is especially important in sprouting seeds and grains. Figure on about 1 level tablespoon of seeds per bird per day; at the beginning of the mating season, increase the amount to 1 heaping tablespoon, and later double or triple that. Several times as much may be needed when the parents are feeding their young.

Rinse the seeds in a sieve under running water to remove dirt, dust, and possible fungus spores or other parasites. Then place the seeds in a jar with some water and keep in a warm room to accelerate swelling. After 12 hours, rinse again thoroughly and then spread out in one layer on a screen. The seeds have to be rinsed and turned several more times before the sprouts break through after 18–24 hours, depending on the temperature. At this point they are ready.

Diet

Sprouts are best offered in a shallow china dish, which should be removed from the aviary after a few hours and washed well before the next use. Never leave uneaten sprouts or sprouts that have fallen to the bottom of the cage or aviary because they rot quickly, especially in the summer, and are an ideal medium in which pathogens may develop.

There is another way of making nutritious fresh food for birds in the winter. Sow some grain, sunflower seeds, or millet in flat dishes with a little soil. When the sprouts are 1–1½ inches (3–4 cm) high, place them in the aviary or cage. Be sure the soil contains no chemicals, such as fertilizer or pesticides.

Animal Proteins

Wild parrots occasionally eat small amounts of food from animal sources. These animal proteins assist the molting process and strengthen the immune system. Food from animal sources is important in the nutrition of captive parrots, too, because it is high in proteins.

A good source of protein is dried prawns. Dried prawns are sometimes used in chicken feed and are usually available at pet stores for a reasonable price. They can be offered in a separate dish or mixed in with the birdseed. Small amounts of cottage cheese, yoghurt, or cheese are also recommended. Some parrots have a craving for cheese, but not too much should be given because it can lead to serious digestive problems.

Canned or dry dog or cat food, if given in moderate amounts, also supplies all the animal protein a parrot needs (about 1 teaspoonful per bird once or twice a week).

Chopped, hard-boiled eggs are high in protein but should be offered only in small amounts because they are hard to digest and can lead to digestive problems if given in excess. (Give about a quarter of an egg per bird twice a week).

Of course, the leftovers of these foods have to be removed promptly. Eating spoiled food (especially dog and cat food) can seriously upset the digestion.

Minerals and Vitamins

The birdseed mixture and other foods just discussed contain most of the minerals a parrot needs. To be sure all nutritional needs are met, however, you should supply a mixture of minerals at regular intervals. Such minerals as phosphorus, calcium, and sodium, as well as the trace elements magnesium, iodine, iron, copper, manganese, and cobalt, are all contained in commercially available calcium supplements. Mixed in with soft foods (cottage cheese or eggs; see Animal Proteins, page 40) or sprinkled on fruit, these supplements prevent mineral deficiencies.

Cuttlebone and blocks of limestone or grit fulfill the same function, but even if they are solidly attached, most large parrots hack them to pieces within a few hours, throw the pieces to the ground, and then ignore them. Sand and grit should always be available. Apart from the mineral content, the tiny pebbles help seed-eating birds, including most parrots, grind down the food in

Diet

their gizzards. Fresh branches from fruit trees, which all parrots like gnawing on, also contain lots of minerals and form a beneficial addition to the diet.

Most vitamins cannot be manufactured by the body and have to be absorbed in food. Parrots that receive a varied diet, including regular doses of sprouts, fruit, and greens, will rarely if ever show symptoms of vitamin deficiency. To make doubly sure, you should give your parrots a multivitamin preparation in the winter, during molting, and during the mating cycle. You can buy multivitamins appropriate for parrots at pet stores. Vitamins in powder form that can be sprinkled over fruit and soft foods are preferable to liquid vitamins, which are often not water soluble and tend to get rancid quickly. Most of the preparations on the market contain vitamins A, C, D, E, and the B group. It is possible to give overdoses of vitamins A and D. Read the instructions on the package carefully, or ask a veterinarian about dosage.

Drinking Water

Most parrots don't drink much, and it is better not to mix medications or vitamins into the drinking water because the amount absorbed is rarely enough to have much positive effect on a disease or deficiency. Drinking water should be available to the bird at all times. Parrots that are completely acclimated (see page 25) can be given their daily drinking water directly from the tap. To improve the quality of the water and to aid the molting process and strengthen the immune system, a few drops of Nutrimin, which contains various mineral supplements, can be added. Parrots that are still in the process of getting acclimated, that is, birds that have only recently left the quarantine station, should get boiled water cooled to lukewarm to which regular tap water is gradually added.

Diseases and How to Keep Parrots Healthy

Once they have adjusted to their new environment, parrots living in captivity usually stay healthy, as long as they are kept and fed properly. Still, they are not immune to sickness, and some diseases to which they are subject can be deadly. In this chapter only those diseases will be discussed that occur relatively frequently and that a parrot keeper should be familiar with in order to take precautions against and, if necessary, initiate treatment for. However, when a parrot actually gets sick, you generally have to consult a veterinarian who knows about birds.

First Signs of Illness and Measures to Take

Birds that are not well exhibit similar symptoms no matter what illness they are suffering from, and it is often impossible to diagnose the exact cause. Sick parrots usually sit in their cage with puffed-up plumage, may sleep for hours during the day, and eat very little or not at all. As soon as you notice these signs (further symptoms are mentioned under the sections on individual diseases in this chapter), you should immediately take the following measures.
• Move the parrot to a small cage, away from the other birds if it lives in an aviary community. If it has to be caught first, approach it as gently as possible. In extreme cases, mere capture can be enough of a shock to a weakened bird to bring on death. (Unfortunately, there is always a danger that giving a bird medicine may have the same fatal consequence.)
• The next thing to do is to expose the parrot to infrared light. Set up the lamp at least 2

feet away from the cage, and aim the light in such a way that the bird can get away from the direct rays (see illustration on this page).
• Substitute weak camomile tea lightly sweetened with glucose for the drinking water, and make available easily digestible soft foods in addition to the birdseed. (Check and keep track of how much the bird eats and drinks!)

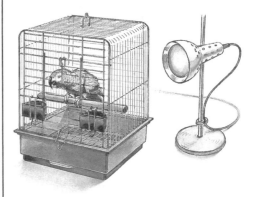

Shining an infrared lamp on a sick bird can have a beneficial effect in treating many diseases. The lamp should be aimed at only half the cage so that the parrot can get away from the warm rays.

• It is a good idea to spread plastic under the perches to catch some droppings for laboratory analysis. As soon as you have a large enough stool sample (about the size of a hazelnut), remove the plastic and take the sample to the veterinarian in a clean jar with a tight lid. Often the laboratory results are available after a few hours.
• Sometimes the general state of the parrot and/or the analysis of the stool sample requires a visit to the veterinarian, who will then determine what should be done. If you

Diseases and How to Keep Parrots Healthy

do have to take your bird, transport it with as little trauma as possible, preferably in a box with solid walls on three sides (see page 25).

Ectoparasites

Infestations with ectoparasites — red bird mites, burrowing mites, feather mites, and lice — rarely take on alarming proportions in parrots that are properly kept. The parasites live on the body surface and in the plumage of the birds.

Symptoms: Infested birds are restless, preen themselves continually, and keep scratching with their feet and toenails because they itch constantly. In time, bald spots appear on the head and abdomen and under the wings.

Prevention: Clean the bird's living quarters thoroughly and regularly, scrubbing all wooden parts well with a brush and hot water.

Treatment: Use a suitable insecticide on both the bird and the cage. Dust the parrot with the powder, and make sure the insecticide penetrates to every corner of the cage. To prevent any chance of poisoning the bird, make sure you observe the following.
• Employ only insecticides bearing an explicit statement by the manufacturer that they are safe for pet birds.
• When you dust the bird, carefully shield its eyes, nostrils, and bill from the powder.
• Never use a spray on birds.
• When you treat the cage or aviary, remove all birds first.

Endoparasites

The most common endoparasites in parrots are tapeworms (Cestoda), roundworms (Ascaridia), and hairworms (Capillaria).

Symptoms: There are no typical symptoms, but the affected birds often sit around with puffed-up feathers, gradually lose weight, and have slimy droppings. Occasionally a parrot will die without warning because the intestine is blocked by hundreds of worms, usually roundworms.

Prevention: Keep the bird's quarters clean. Prompt treatment reduces the severity and harm of a worm infestation. Aviculturists who keep their parrots in outdoor aviaries should have the birds' droppings checked for signs of worms several times a year. Sending in a stool sample for laboratory analysis should be routine procedure whenever a bird first exhibits general signs of illness (see page 42).

Treatment: Use only worm medication prescribed by a veterinarian (Piperzine or Levamisole, and in cases of tapeworms, Yomesan). Follow the veterinarian's directions faithfully; an overdose is dangerous to the bird.

Inflammation of the Intestines

Intestinal infections, or enteritis, are one of the most common health problems of parrots. Possible causes that trigger them are changes in diet, poor nutrition, tumors, absorption of poisonous substances, colds, parasite infestation, bacterial infections (*Escherichia coli* and *Salmonella*), fungi, and viruses.

Symptoms: In addition to the general signs of illness mentioned on page 42, there may be diarrhea and — because diarrhea leads to loss of fluids — dehydration. Enteritis is also accompanied by loss of appetite, and the resulting condition is serious and possibly life-threatening.

43

Diseases and How to Keep Parrots Healthy

Reminder: Some psychic factors can affect the digestion of parrots and lead to diarrhealike droppings, which, however, should not be mistaken for symptoms of enteritis. A raptor bird circling in the air overhead or a cat crouching nearby apparently ready to pounce may cause sudden diarrhea, as may the panic felt by the bird when caught by the keeper or a sudden confrontation with rival birds.

Treatment: Give the affected bird camomile tea, Kaopectate, or Pepto-Bismol, and easily digestible food, and expose it to even warmth (see First Signs of Illness and Measures to Take, page 42). If the parrot appears seriously weakened, take it to the veterinarian as quickly as possible and take along a stool sample. Any medication for this condition (usually a broad-spectrum antibiotic) has to be prescribed by a veterinarian. Follow the veterinarian's directions carefully!

Salmonellosis (Paratyphoid Infection)

Food or water contaminated with salmonellae causes salmonellosis. The disease can also be transmitted by such carriers as wild birds, especially city pigeons, rats, mice, and flies that live in or near the aviaries and introduce pathogens in their droppings.

Symptoms: There are no characteristic symptoms beyond the general ones. Only a laboratory analysis of the droppings can show whether salmonellae are present.

Treatment: Give a broad-spectrum antibiotic (nitrofurazone or furazolidone) but only on advice of a veterinarian and in accordance with directions.

Reminder: Because salmonellosis can be transmitted to humans, take proper precautions when handling sick birds.

Coccidiosis

Coccidia are microscopic protozoans that live in the mucous membranes of the parrot's intestines.

Symptoms: Coccidia cause serious inflammation of the intestines and may lead to intestinal bleeding. The condition is accompanied by diarrhea and loss of weight.

Prevention: Clean and disinfect the parrot's quarters thoroughly and regularly; have the (sometimes bloody) droppings checked. Early detection is important because birds can get rid of coccidia quickly if treatment is begun promptly.

Treatment: Only a veterinarian can describe appropriate medication (sulfa drugs).

Trichomoniasis

This is an infection caused by a microscopic protozoan called a trichomonad. The infection is hardly ever acute in mature parrots, but it can be passed on to, and take on active form in, nestlings fed from the parent's crop.

Symptoms: In the acute form of this disease, a thick, yellowish coating covers the mucous membranes of the mouth and crop, interfering with food intake and even with breathing.

Treatment: The veterinarian can give you effective medications (dimetridazole) for both prevention and treatment.

Diseases and How to Keep Parrots Healthy

Crop Inflammation

The ingestion of dirty water, spoiled or unsuitable food, or things not meant to be eaten can lead to an inflammation of the mucous membranes in the crop. The inflammation may be caused by poisonous substances or by fermentation in the crop, as well as by pathogens (bacteria, fungi, or trichomonads) that are often present in healthy birds but that can cause inflammation if the general resistance is lowered.

Symptoms: In addition to the usual general signs of illness, you may observe loss of appetite and vomiting of a viscid, brownish white slime that gradually turns the plumage of the head dirty and sticky.

Treatment: Consult the veterinarian for effective treatment and medication. Administer Maalox or DiGel to soothe the crop and neutralize the acid.

Disorders of the Respiratory System

Respiratory problems can arise from a variety of causes. Some of them are bacteria, viruses, or fungi in the respiratory system and colds caused by drafts, wrong temperature, or sudden changes in temperature. A specific diagnosis is extremely difficult and often possible only postmortem.

Symptoms: General symptoms of illness as well as frequent sneezing, wet or plugged nostrils, discharge from the nostrils, noisy breathing, and breathing difficulties (the bird sits with feet planted far apart, breathing through the open beak, and whipping the tail up and down visibly at every breath). Sometimes the eyelids and conjunctiva are inflamed.

Obvious signs of respiratory disorders are breathing with an open beak and wet or stuffed-up nostrils.

Prevention: Keep the bird under optimal conditions.

Treatment: The most effective measure seems to be intensive treatment with a heat lamp (see page 42). If the condition does not improve after 24 hours, however, consulting a veterinarian is imperative. If there are obvious breathing difficulties and noisy breathing, the parrot should be taken to the veterinarian immediately. Early treatment enhances the chances for cure, but not all cases respond to treatment.

Aspergillosis

Aspergillosis is an infection caused by molds and affects primarily young birds and those weakened by age. It attacks the respiratory system because the pathogen is normally inhaled. Of the large parrots, those of the genus *Pionus* seem to be most prone to this disease.

Symptoms: The major symptom is abnormal breathing, which does not, however, become apparent until the disease has reached an advanced stage.

Diseases and How to Keep Parrots Healthy

Prevention: Keep the birds under optimal conditions. Poor hygiene, mass conditions, spoiled food, heat, and moisture all foster the growth and spreading of mold. Breeders should be especially careful during the mating season to provide the right kind of litter in the nest boxes. Although some breeders favor damp peat moss as litter, I do not recommend it because aspergillus flourishes in it. More suitable are excelsior and sawdust from coniferous trees, both of which discourage the growth of mold.

Treatment: The mortality rate of birds with aspergillosis is high. Treatment is complicated and expensive and requires a veterinarian knowledgeable about bird diseases.

Parrot Fever (Psittacosis)

Parrot fever is an infectious disease, caused by an intracellular parasite, *Chlamydia*, that, despite its name, is not limited to parrots. The parasites causing it have been found in more than 100 other bird species (that is, birds not belonging to the parrot family), and the term "ornithosis" is used when birds other than parrots are affected.

In the early 1930s, severe outbreaks of psittacosis were observed in Europe as well as in America, and when it was found that the disease can take on epidemic proportions and can spread to humans, the importation and sale of psittacine birds became subject to strict regulations both in Europe and in the United States. Restrictions have since been relaxed, but because of the quarantine period and prophylactic treatment mandatory for newly imported birds, most of the parrots sold are free of the disease and the virus responsible for it. Nevertheless, some danger remains because of bird-smuggling operations and occasional laxity on the part of some mass dealers in following quarantine regulations.

Symptoms: As with many other diseases, the onset of psittacosis is not marked by clear symptoms. Drowsiness, loss of weight, watery green droppings, conjunctivitis, and lack of appetite can all be secondary symptoms.

Prevention: Proper nutrition and keeping the birds under optimal conditions minimize the risk of an outbreak of psittacosis but offer no absolute safeguard. If the symptoms mentioned occur, have a stool sample analyzed. Once the condition is acute, the pathogens can be detected. Be wary of buying parrots from a mass breeder. (Detailed discussions of psittacosis can be found in various books and other publications; see Useful Literature and Addresses, page 141.)

Treatment: Any incidence of psittacosis has to be reported to the public health authorities. The sick birds are then quarantined according to official health regulations and treated with tetracycline drugs. Usually the medication is mixed with the soft food, but it can also be given in the form of injections. Very rarely, birds do recover from the disease without medical treatment, but they are then carriers and can infect not only other birds but people as well.

Psittacosis can be life threatening in humans. In light cases the illness resembles a cold or the flu and has similar symptoms, but in more serious attacks the patient suffers from high fever and respiratory infection. In humans, as in birds, the disease responds to drugs if it is diagnosed and treated in time.

Diseases and How to Keep Parrots Healthy

Avitaminosis-B$_6$ (Vitamin B Deficiency)

"Avitaminosis" is a general term for diseases caused by deficiency of one or more vitamins. Avitaminosis-B — a deficiency of vitamins of the B complex — deserves special mention because it affects the nervous system and often takes a peculiar form in birds.

Symptoms: Apart from general weakness, avitaminosis-B manifests itself in paralysis of the toes and legs and, in advanced stages, in compulsive, unnatural movements and twisting of the head.

Prevention: Ordinarily, birds get enough B vitamins in their normal food (see Diet, page 35), but prolonged storage or freezing causes the vitamins to deteriorate. Check the packing date when you buy bird food (see page 36), and check the viability of the seeds (see page 36).

There is a direct connection between vitamin B deficiency and the presence of parasites. Intestinal parasites, especially coccidia, destroy B vitamins, and an explosive increase of coccidia can thus lead to an acute vitamin-B deficiency. This is one reason that parrots infested with parasites should receive treatment as promptly as possible (see page 43).

Treatment: Ask your veterinarian or pet dealer for the name of an effective vitamin-B supplement (follow directions for amounts, although an overdose is highly unlikely). To be on the safe side, have the veterinarian examine the bird because the symptoms already mentioned can also signal other illnesses, such as infections or poisoning.

Rickets

Rickets is a metabolic disorder caused by a shortage of vitamin D, calcium, and phosphorus in the diet of young birds.

Symptoms: If the above-mentioned nutrients are not available in sufficient amounts while the birds are growing up, the skeleton does not form properly. The long, hollow bones are especially affected, the birds with rickets usually have bent legs with thick joints. Curvature of the spine and of the sternum may also occur but are revealed only through x-rays. Depending on the severity of the condition, the birds may be unable to sit up straight on a perch or on the ground. At a more advanced stage, they lie helplessly on the ground, unable to move their feet. At this point treatment is probably too late because increased intake of vitamins and minerals merely solidifies the bones in their twisted shapes and the bird is permanently crippled.

Prevention and treatment: Supply the birds, especially when there are young ones, with a source of minerals in which calcium and phosphorus are present in the right proportions. Ordinary bird calcium will take care of all mineral and trace element requirements of captive birds. Supplements that can be added to the drinking water are also acceptable.

Feather Plucking

Feather plucking leaves a bird unsightly and should probably be considered a psychic disorder.

Symptoms: The severity of the condition can range from occasional plucking and biting of a feather here and there — mostly

Diseases and How to Keep Parrots Healthy

on the shoulders and the breast — to the systematic pulling of the entire plumage, leaving the bird entirely naked (except for the head, where the bill cannot reach). There have even been incidents of self-mutilation in which birds have chewed on their own skin and muscle tissue.

Possible causes: Feather plucking is relatively common among large parrots and primarily affects birds kept singly.

The underlying causes are not fully understood, but a combination of several factors seems to encourage it. These factors are
• Insufficient opportunity for exercise (as in a small cage)
• Boredom (if quarters are too "sterile")
• Continual stress (in an overcrowded aviary)
• Lack or loss of a human partner (especially in the case of birds kept singly)
• Absence of a sexual partner at the onset of sexual maturity (especially in the case of birds kept in aviaries or for breeding purposes)
• Skin disorders that cause itching
• Improper diet, wrong temperature, and low humidity
• Lack of bathing opportunity or regular showers

Treatment: Correct conditions of housing and/or improve diet. In many cases the obvious solution is to move the affected bird from a cage to a larger aviary or to give it things to keep busy with, like branches for nibbling and toys. If possible, introduce a partner of the same species. Spend more time playing with a single bird. Commercial remedies for feather plucking are generally useless. Putting a collar of plastic (Elizabethan collar) or some other material around a bird's neck can stop the feather plucking and gives the plumage a chance to grow back in. This is by no means a permanent cure. In many cases the collar (which must always be put on by a veterinarian) only aggravates the psychic malady.

Egg Binding

We speak of egg binding when a hen is unable to pass a fully formed, mature egg.

Symptoms: The hen may be generally miserable as she tries to lay the egg by pressing down with all her might. Often she extrudes large droppings mixed with blood and emits soft cheeps of pain.

Causes:
• In very young birds, the sexual organs may not yet be fully developed and the pelvis may still be too narrow.
• Poor housing conditions and improper diet (cold, wetness, lack of room for exercise, or vitamin deficiencies).
• Eggs that are oversize or have shells that are too rough or too soft.
• Abnormalities or inflammation of the oviduct.
• Hormonal imbalance.
• Overbreeding.
• Calcium deficiency.
• Diseases.

Prevention: Ensure an optimal diet and environment, especially during the mating period.

Treatment: To alleviate the pain, you can lightly massage the bird's lower belly with some warm oil. This is only a first-aid measure; take the bird to the veterinarian as quickly as you can. If the egg remains stuck in the cloaca too long, the hen may die of exhaustion. After the emergency is over, exposure to an infrared lamp has been found to aid recuperation.

Names of Body Parts and Plumage

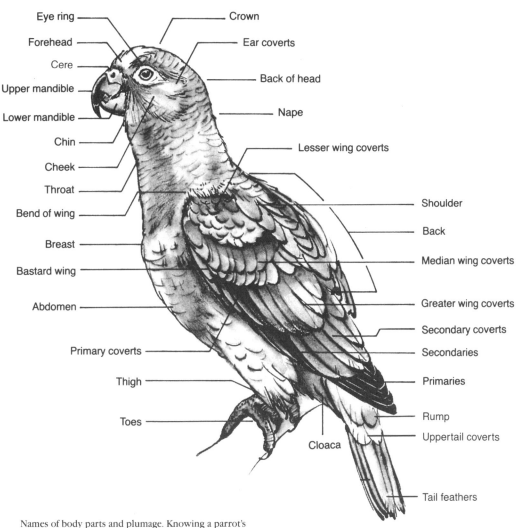

Eye ring — Crown

Forehead — Ear coverts

Cere

Upper mandible — Back of head

Lower mandible — Nape

Chin

Cheek — Lesser wing coverts

Throat

Bend of wing — Shoulder

Breast — Back

Bastard wing — Median wing coverts

Abdomen — Greater wing coverts

Primary coverts — Secondary coverts

Thigh — Secondaries

Toes — Primaries

Cloaca — Rump

Uppertail coverts

Tail feathers

Names of body parts and plumage. Knowing a parrot's anatomy and the names of various parts of its plumage is useful not only for conversations with the veterinarian but also for recognizing different kinds of parrots (see Popular Parrot Species, page 95).

Raising Parrots

Many of the parrot species commonly available through the pet trade have thus far failed to reproduce in captivity or have produced offspring only rarely. The parrots in the cages and aviaries of fanciers as well as those found in pet stores are usually — and always have been — imported animals. If we look at the situation in our parrots' native lands, we realize that soon it will be indefensible, if not impossible, to continue buying parrots taken from the wild. This is why I devote so much space in this chapter to detailed information and practical advice on how to raise parrots successfully. I want to urge parrot fanciers not only to keep large parrots for pleasure but also to raise them.

Parrots — a Group of Birds Threatened by Extinction

The wild populations of many parrot species have been decimated, as have those of many other animals and plants. The major reason for this is the vast destruction of habitat. To state it more concretely, the parrots' very basis of life is being destroyed. The trees in which they build their nests and that furnish them with food are knocked down by huge bulldozers that work away in the forests day after day and fell between 50 and 75 acres per minute or upward of 50,000 square miles of trees every year — trees that have been growing for many decades — for the sake of the wood and to create arable land. (Whether and to what extent the cutting down of the rain forests benefits the poor people in those countries is a subject we cannot broach here.) In any case, the destruction of natural habitat and, in some areas of the world, the "over-harvesting" of wild parrots to supply the pet trade have brought many parrot species to the brink of extinction.

The Washington Convention

Scientists, environmentalists, and politicians of many nations met for the first time in 1973 in Washington, D.C., to discuss the threat of extinction to plants and animals and, if possible, to reverse the trend. The outcome of this conference was the Convention on International Trade in Endangered Species of Wild Fauna and Flora (CITES), often referred to as the Washington Convention. This document lists all endangered plants and animals under three categories reflecting the severity of danger, and the regulations contained in it affecting trade in wild fauna and flora are binding for the countries that sign the Convention.

Of practical consequence to parrot fanciers is that since the third convention of March 8, 1981, all parrots, with the exception of budgerigars, cockatiels, and alexandrine parakeets, have been listed as endangered, most of them in Appendix II to the Convention. Species in this category can be sold only if a legal export permit (from the country of origin) and an import permit can be produced. Most parrots at pet stores do have the required papers and belong to species listed in Appendix II of the Washington Convention. Applications for exporting and importing parrots are denied more and more often, however, and the number of different species available for sale keeps shrinking. These restrictions grow out of an effort to preserve the decimated parrot populations

Raising Parrots

as much as the continual encroachment on their natural habitat permits.

Some of the species listed in Endangered and Extinct Species (see page 138) are close to extinction, and trade in them is illegal. Birds belonging to this group that turn up occasionally have been smuggled into the country, were bred in captivity, or were imported before the regulation in question took effect. Existing federal regulations require that every captive-bred and wild-caught bird entering the United States, pass a U.S. Department of Agriculture (USDA) quarantine as well as Fish & Wildlife Service and Customs Service. If forbidden birds are found, they may be confiscated and stiff fines may be imposed on the importer. Don't be tempted, therefore, if you are vacationing in an exotic spot, to try to find some rare parrot and smuggle it through customs.

The Aviculturist's Role in Preserving Parrots

Our efforts to propagate parrots in captivity should be seen in the light of what I have just discussed. It is more important now than ever before for us to create conditions in our aviaries that are optimal for reproduction. Every parrot that is born in captivity means that one less bird has to be removed from the wild to satisfy the growing demand for pet parrots. This is why I urge you so strongly to encourage your parrots to reproduce. Even a tame pet parrot that has learned to talk can produce offspring, and the bird is no less lovable even though it may shift its attention away from its keeper to other parrots.

The breeding of parrots is not comparable to that of other pets or even smaller cage birds. Parrots have not become domesticated to the extent that their reproduction can be planned and genetically manipulated as it often is in domestic animals. On the contrary, conditions have to be just so for a pair of parrots to show interest in mating at all, which can be very frustrating to the owner. Still, things have changed since the days when the birth of young parrots was simply a matter of luck. Now systematic efforts to breed

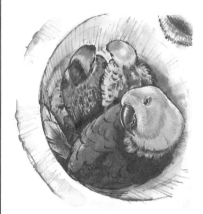

Female eclectus parrot with two young in the nest. The hen leaves the nest only rarely until the nestlings start eating on their own at about 12–13 weeks.

parrots are showing success with increasing frequency. In fact, some parrots of the Pacific distribution — primarily eclectus parrots, but also cockatoos (the greater and the lesser sulfur-crested and the rose-breasted) — now are bred in captivity quite regularly. Of the African species, both races of the gray parrot have been raised by many fanciers.

51

Raising Parrots

The situation is more problematic with South American parrots, which demand special conditions if they are to show interest in breeding. All in all, we seem to be on the verge of entering the age of "systematic parrot breeding." The number of birds bred thus far is still too small, however, to have a significant impact on the import business.

This chapter is for those who realize that breeding parrots takes enormous patience, runs into money, and — last but not least — depends on luck but who are still willing to try. In the following sections I attempt to give enough information to help avoid major mistakes and years of disappointment. It may already be too late to save certain parrot species from extinction, but any breeding success is at least a step in the right direction.

The Housing of Breeder Birds

Even though parrots occasionally produce offspring under adverse conditions (as in a small cage with an attached nest box), anyone intent on breeding these birds should provide optimal housing for them, whether that means adapting the quarters the birds already inhabit or building a new structure. A large outdoor aviary with a shelter that has plenty of light and can be heated or, in other words, a combined indoor-outdoor aviary as described on page 21, is the ideal setting for parrots to breed in. In fact, such a setup is a must for successful parrot breeding. To be sure, one can raise parrots in large indoor aviaries, but in my opinion this only works if the keeper makes a special effort to provide everything the birds need (lighting, heat, and nutrition). Attempts to

breed parrots in small indoor aviaries are not very promising, and only luck will produce the desired result. If you have the opportunity to visit the establishment of an experienced parrot breeder who has had more than occasional success, you will probably find that the birds not only receive optimal care but are also housed in spacious indoor-outdoor aviaries rather than a shack in the backyard.

Some Important Factors in Housing Breeder Birds

Birds that are expected to breed should not be exposed to too many distractions. This is why the following rules should be observed.
• Every pair that has formed a mating bond should have a separate aviary.
• Single birds have to be removed from the aviary and housed somewhere else; they would create trouble in the aviary and keep the other birds from breeding. It is best to move them out of sight and earshot.
• Avoid housing two pairs of the same species next to each other. Sometimes the males in neighboring aviaries drive each other to fury and thus interfere in the brooding.
• Keep wandering cats and dogs away from the aviaries because the sight of them will put the birds into a state of alarm.
• Explain to your children — and to others if they are around — that they must not play next to the aviaries or run past them, let alone rattle the grating, because the birds need peace and quiet to raise their young.
• You yourself, as a proud parrot breeder, may prove a nuisance to the birds if you keep running to the aviary to check on progress or to show the parrots off to visitors. I

receive occasional visits from aspiring or actual parrot owners, and I am usually happy to show them my setup, as long as they approach the birds quietly and calmly, but not while the birds are sitting on their eggs. I think, however, that parrot owners who keep all visitors away from their birds and enter the aviary only at certain times of day and in clothing the birds know go too far. These birds will be frightened by the slightest deviation from their normal routine, which is surely not desirable. I do know of cases in which parrots could be induced to reproduce only under such conditions. The Moluccan cockatoo is one of these extrasensitive parrots. It has reproduced in captivity only on rare occasions and only when secluded as described. (When kept singly, this cockatoo accepts humans very quickly and can be a charming and friendly pet.)

• The proximity of a busy highway with loud traffic noise during the day and bright headlights at night will have a detrimental effect on the birds' willingness or ability to reproduce. The same is true if you live near an airport or a military base. There are always exceptions to the rule, however. I met a parrot fancier in Muensterland, West Germany (near a NATO airfield), whose birds were subjected daily to sonic booms from military jets "without blinking an eye." They would sit in the aviary with perfect composure, look up into the sky when an airplane appeared, and not react in any way to the deafening noise. Students of behavior are familiar with this phenomenon and use the terms "habituation" and "waning of response to stimulus" to describe it. In lay language we would say that the birds get used to a recurrent event and learn that the boom accompanying the breaking of the sound barrier signifies no danger to them. I still doubt whether the birds would maintain their composure if they were sitting on eggs.

Sexing Parrots

Accurate sexing of birds is important if you want to match pairs for mating. Sexing parrots varies in difficulty with different species and is in some cases possible only through a technical procedure at considerable expense. The gender of parrots from the Pacific distribution can usually be determined on the basis of external characteristics. Very few African and South African parrots can be sexed with any degree of certainty on the basis of appearance. Endoscopy, a medical procedure (see page 58), is a scientifically accurate method of determining sex, but there are a few other more or less reliable clues that will interest a parrot owner.

Reliable Clues
Cockatoos: All cockatoos described in this book, except the bare-eyed cockatoo, can be sexed on the basis of eye color. Ornithologists have found that the iris of males is dark brown to black, whereas that of females is lighter brown to rust brown. In Moluccans the difference is not always immediately apparent, but when a small light, like a pencil flashlight, is briefly aimed at the eye, the difference can easily be seen here, too. (By contrast, both male and female bare-eyed Cockatoos have black irises.) As the birds get older, the eye color of most species becomes more distinct, making it easier to tell the gender.

Raising Parrots

Eclectus parrots: There is a clear difference between the sexes in all ten subspecies of this parrot (page 105) — an almost unheard of situation with parrots. The males of all ten subspecies are basically green, whereas the females, depending on the subspecies, are red with either blue or purple markings. (Eclectus parrots are also the only species in which the female is gaudier than the male.) Because in all other parrots the female is either the same color as the male or more muted, red and green eclectus parrots used to be considered two separate species. The ornithologist A. B. Meyer was the first to prove, in 1884, that they were the male and female of the same species.

Partially Reliable Clues

Other parrots have less striking external sex differences that can help determine the gender. Some of them apply to cockatoos and eclectus parrots as well but play only a minor role here because of the more obvious differences mentioned above. Each of the characteristics I'm about to mention can be relied on only partially and is not necessarily found in every case. A combination of several of them increases the likelihood that the assigned sex is correct.

- Male parrots are, as a rule, larger than females.
- Male parrots have a bigger head and bill than females.
- Seen in profile, the face of a male looks long and straight; that of a female is smaller, shorter, and rounder.
- A fully grown male parrot usually weighs 10 — 15% more than a female.

- The male sits upright, a female, more slumped. Sometimes the female practically lies on the perch.
- The pelvic bones of a female are farther apart than those of a male. As a result, the feet of a male are closer together than the female's in a normal sitting position (see illustration on page 57).
- The different color areas of the plumage are less distinctly delineated in females.
- In males, the characteristic markings of the species tend to be brighter and larger than in females.
- The courtship behavior of males is often more pronounced than that of females. Mature males are more often seen with their tails spread, their neck feathers raised, and assuming an upright, "strutting" pose.
- Females often indicate their readiness to mate by leaning forward and practically "lying" on a perch. They stay in that position, with slightly raised, quivering wings, for several seconds. This behavior also occurs in females that are temporarily without a mate.

These ten clues apply to the parrots mentioned below. For individual genera and species, the following points should also be taken into consideration.

Poicephalus **parrots:** In Senegal parrots and related species, the variations in color intensity on the breast should probably be regarded as a sign of different races rather

Blue and gold macaws preening each other. One bird is ▷ reaching its rump up to its partner to have the feathers smoothed.

than as a secondary sex characteristic. Male Senegal parrots often have exceptionally large bills.

One parrot fancier has observed that the yellow band on the head of brown parrots is wider in females than in males (see page 108). Male Jardine's parrots have very big bills.

Gray parrots: The literature on these parrots mentions a number of different and often mutually contradictory signs for determining the gender of both subspecies, but there is nothing definitive to add to the ten clues already listed.

Amazons: Of the Amazons described in this book (see page 111), the only species in which the plumage differs for the two genders is the spectacled Amazon. In this species the bend of the wing is red in males and green in females.

The rules or clues already listed are all you have to go on for other Amazons. Special caution is in order, however. I have seen individual cases in which Amazons showed just the opposite sex characteristics from what you would expect; in other words, males exhibited more or less "typical" female characteristics, and vice versa.

***Pionus* parrots:** The shape of the eye rings seems to distinguish the two sexes in red-vented and bronze-winged parrots. According to my observations, the area of

bare skin around the eyes is generally round in males and elongated or oval in females.

Caiques: Both black-headed and the white-bellied caiques are extremely difficult to sex since neither their external appearance nor their behavior gives any clues.

Sexing parrots. Females, like the bird on the right, often sit on a perch with feet wider apart than males.

Macaws: The huge size of the beak makes quite evident which are the males in the large-sized species. A number of fanciers maintain that the beak's shape differs, too. The upper mandible of the female, they have observed, is more sickle-shaped than that of the male, which is longer and straighter but with a more pronounced curve at the tip. In hyacinth macaws I have noticed that the bare elastic skin at the base of the lower mandible often changes color in the female during the mating season (this is true also of single birds when they are in a mating mood). This skin, which is ordinarily yellowish orange, then changes to a pale yellowish white.

◁ Parrot behavior.
Above left: The beak is tucked in the back feathers for sleeping. Above right: Parrots hold on to big morsels of food with their feet. Below: This tame blue and gold macaw likes to juggle with a plate.

Raising Parrots

Endoscopy

All the methods of sexing parrots thus far mentioned have one thing in common: They are not foolproof. Veterinarians have tried to get around this problem by resorting to a diagnostic procedure that has long been used in human medicine but was first applied in veterinary medicine only in the mid-1970s. In this procedure, known as endoscopy, the interior of the body is examined by introducing a tiny mirror with a light into the body cavity. Endoscopy has been used successfully in sexing parrots for a number of years.

Depending on how many birds are to be examined, the cost runs somewhere between $50 and $60 per bird. The operation is performed at colleges of veterinary medicine and by veterinarians familiar with the procedure.

The bird to be operated on is briefly anesthetized. Then a small incision is made below the last rib in the left side. Through this opening the endoscope is inserted, which, if there are no anatomic abnormalities, exposes the internal sexual organs to view: testes in males, ovaries in females. The examination reveals not only the bird's sex but also the state of the sex organs (active, the bird will be ready to mate soon; passive, no offspring are to be expected for the time being) and any sign of disease in the internal organs.

This procedure has become refined over the last few years and now carries practically no risks. When the bird awakens from the operation it should not be returned to the aviary right away but should be kept in a small cage and carefully observed for 2 or 3 days.

For a long time I objected to this method of sexing parrots because I felt that the stress it imposed on the birds was not justifiable on ethical grounds. After years of scruples I finally decided to have at least my Amazons sexed through endoscopy. In view of the advances in medical technology on the one hand and, on the other, the imperative to try to preserve some of the endangered parrot species, I felt I had to overcome my reservations. After all, it is hardly in the birds' interest if out of ignorance we keep them for years with partners of their own sex while the next cage might house a potential "real" partner.

Sexual Maturity and Determining a Bird's Age

In the smaller species of the parrot family the completion of the first year usually brings sexual maturity. Larger parrots do not reach this stage until they are 3 years old. The general rule for all the parrots described in this book is that offspring may be expected at the earliest in the spring of a bird's fourth year. Some of the smaller parrots, like the long-winged parrots of Africa, may raise young during their third year. Many macaws wait until their fifth or sixth year.

Being able to ascertain the age of a newly acquired bird is obviously of practical importance to a parrot owner. There are a number of fairly reliable clues for telling a juvenile bird *up to about 2 years of age.*

Bill: Young parrots have smooth, shiny bills; in older birds the accumulation of thin, horny plates (parrots' bills never stop growing) give the bill a less regular appearance.

Raising Parrots

Legs and toes: The skin pattern on the legs and toes becomes coarse with age, and the epidermis grows thicker. In fully grown birds the horny plates are clearly visible on the toes, whereas these plates are still very fine in younger birds.

Eyes: In many parrots eye color helps determine age. Almost all juvenile parrots have dark (gray, brown, or black) irises that usually lighten with age. The change is particularly clear in Senegal and gray parrots. At about 10 months the orange-brown eyes of Senegals turn orange, and in grays the grayish irises become straw colored. With increasing age the eye color becomes more distinct.

Sexing parrots. In large macaws the head and bill of the males are often more massive than those of the females. Seen in profile, a male's face looks long and straight; that of the female, short and somewhat rounder.

Size and plumage: Juveniles are usually smaller than adults of their species; their plumage is more muted, and the markings are not set off as sharply. With increasing age the markings grow bigger and deepen in color.

Reminder: At this point the best we can do is to distinguish in general between immature and adult birds. It would be useful to be able to tell the difference between, say, a 3-year-old and an 8-year-old bird. Even to make an educated guess of this sort, however, takes extensive experience and the chance to compare many birds.

Buying Breeder Birds

When you buy birds you hope to breed you have to watch out for a few more things than when you are looking for "ordinary" parrots to keep for pleasure only (see page 12). Just putting two birds of opposite gender together in an aviary — after having sexed them correctly — does not necessarily lead to mating and offspring (see Matching Pairs, page 62). As a parrot breeder you should be aware that the birds' earlier history has a bearing on their reproductive behavior.

Young Imported Parrots

If you have bought your parrots from a pet dealer or an importer, you should be prepared for a long waiting period. These are usually immature birds that will not reach sexual maturity for some time (see Sexual Maturity and Determining a Bird's Age, page 58). Even if they are old enough to breed, they will be too busy getting used to their new way of life, including different food and living in a cage, to think about breeding. It will take them many weeks or months to adjust to captivity and learn to trust their caretaker. They also have to go through their first molt in captivity, which temporarily weakens them. Eventually the birds, with their frayed feathers and clipped wing and

Raising Parrots

tail feathers, will metamorphose into beautiful, shiny parrots that can fly again.

Parrots have to be 3 or 4 years old — depending on the species — before they go through the first courtship ritual, and the first eggs are not laid until the hen is 4 or 5 years old. In most cases two parrots (obviously of opposite sex) that have lived together since they were juveniles get along well and form a sexual bond.

Acclimated Older Parrots

Sometimes older, completely acclimated parrots that are used to life in a cage or aviary and to a human caretaker are advertised in avicultural magazines or local newspapers. (On rare occasions such birds are also available through pet dealers.) Such birds are for sale for one of three reasons.

• The parrot was kept as a pet. It may be quite tame and able to "talk," but the owner has gotten tired of having a parrot around and is trying to sell the bird. These parrots tend to be expensive because the seller would like to get something back for the time put into training the bird.

• The seller is a serious breeder who, after matching pairs, has some birds left over. He or she may have acquired a number of parrots of the same species, and after most of them have paired the seller is left with a few perfectly healthy and perhaps sexually mature birds he or she now wants to sell. These parrots are often still quite wild and have adjusted only partly to a human caretaker. Birds like these may be relatively inexpensive because the owner is not out to make a profit but simply wants to get rid of the birds without financial loss.

• A third category of people try to sell birds with defects — some apparent and some not — under the label of "good breeding stock." This is where special caution is in order. It is not uncommon for parrots to be offered for sale that seem to be healthy and cheerful but are in fact not of breeding quality because they are infertile or suffer from behavioral abnormalities that keep them from mating.

The so-called breeding pairs that one often sees advertised may be ill-matched pairs that have repeatedly failed to reproduce. The keeper has finally given up and wants to get rid of them. I know of cases in which two male cockatoos were advertised as "breeding pairs" (cockatoos are easy to sex) and males were offered for sale as females. Questionable sales practices are of course not restricted to the bird trade, and one runs into dishonest salespeople in other business dealings. Aviculturists with years of experience gradually get to know the "black sheep" in the trade and conduct business only with reputable dealers. If you are just starting out with parrots, I suggest that you get in touch with an experienced parrot fancier or with a breeders' club (see Useful Literature and Addresses, page 141) to get the name of a reputable source of parrots.

Buying mature, healthy birds from a domestic source has the advantage of a much shorter waiting period. Adult parrots, however, are often more reluctant to accept mates and there may be initial problems synchronizing the mating cycles because the birds enter the courtship and mating mood at different times.

Raising Parrots

If you buy an older parrot, you hardly ever have to worry that the bird might be past breeding age. Most parrots living in captivity grow very old, and there are documented cases of large parrots still producing off-spring at 30 years of age.

Young Domestically Raised Parrots

Parrots bred in captivity are in great demand and, unfortunately, in short supply. These birds are already used to living in captivity and are therefore likely to reproduce under these conditions. It is too bad that breeders sometimes, depending on how rare the species is, ask incredibly overinflated prices that, in my opinion, are not worth paying. Domestically raised young parrots, like imported ones, need several years to become sexually mature. The bright side of this is that the years two young parrots spend growing up together tend to foster a harmonious relationship that later leads to mating.

Should You Try to Mate Parrots That Are Kept Singly?

There is no simple yes or no to the question of whether parrots that have lived as pets in the midst of a human family are suitable candidates for breeding. The opinions of breeders about the "usefulness" of these birds varies greatly. Some say that pet birds are too much "imprinted" to humans to be able to accept other members of their species as mates. Others think they are simply too old, and still others see no reason they should not be bred.

I personally think that the truth, as in so many cases, lies somewhere in the middle.

In answer to the first opinion, one could object that no parrot that was originally imported is imprinted to humans and that birds bred the natural way — that is, birds that are raised by their parents — have probably retained their natural instincts.

Scientists who study animal behavior — ethologists — use the word *imprinting* to describe a learning process that occurs in earliest infancy and leaves permanent, indeed, often indelible results. Prime examples are sexual imprinting and learning what territory is home or what kind of creature to follow. During a certain, usually very short period, the so-called sensitive phase, the young animal permanently acquires all the knowledge necessary for survival, including what a future mate looks like. We have a detailed understanding of imprinting only for a few kinds of animals. The work of the Austrian Nobel Prize winner Konrad Lorenz is widely known. The results of his study of greylag geese, which led to his discovery of neonatal imprinting in animals, have been published variously in popularized form, including in school textbooks, some of which include "The Story of Martina the Gosling." More recently, other birds have been studied in connection with the imprinting theory. I am thinking in particular of zebra finches, on which the German ethologist Klaus Immelmann and Matthew M. Vriends have published some interesting studies (see Barron's pet owners manual *Zebra Finches*, by H.-J. Martin).

No such information is available about large parrots, and we will probably have to wait a long time for it because of the scarcity of baby parrots to be observed in captivity.

Raising Parrots

We can safely assume that imported parrots are at least 4–5 months old when sold and thus well past imprinting. These birds may develop a close relationship with their keeper, but no real imprinting takes place. Sooner or later these parrots, even if they have been surrounded exclusively by humans, will want to mate with members of their own species. I admit that the transition

Parrots that have formed a close bond often go through the same motions at the same time. In this picture, two rose-breasted cockatoos are stretching their left wings and fanning their tails simultaneously.

from being an only bird in a human family to life in an aviary community may not be all smooth sailing. I certainly do not agree with people who claim that a tame caged bird can be turned into a breeder without any problems. You simply have to try and see what happens.

The objection that pet parrots are too old for breeding is justified only in the rarest of cases. As mentioned on page 61, we know of 30-year-old parrots that have reproduced.

Matching Pairs

People often forget that after considering age, gender, sexual maturity, state of health, and origin of parrots they hope to breed, they have to take account of one more factor. Parrots can be very choosy about accepting a mate. Birds living in captivity only rarely have an opportunity to "select" a partner as they would in nature. There are still ways to offer them something like a "free choice." If you have enough space and the necessary financial resources, you should purchase several (about six to eight) parrots of the same species and keep them together in a community aviary until they reach sexual maturity. This gives them a chance to pick a partner out of a small group. You can tell quite quickly when one or more pairs have formed. Two birds that have taken a liking to each other sit close together, fly together from branch to branch, eat together, and preen each other's head and rump. If the birds were sexed by endoscopy immediately after purchase and banded with different colors, it will then be easy to make sure that the pairs are heterosexual.

You may wonder why I mention the need of checking for heterosexuality. Parrots that live in captivity, where they rarely have a wide range of choice for partners, often bond with members of their own sex. These pairs often behave exactly like a true pair, one bird taking on the male, the other the female role.

The larger the flock that is temporarily assembled to promote pairing, the smaller is the chance that birds will choose others of their own sex for mates. Knowing the sex of all your birds is always helpful, however.

Raising Parrots

If two birds in a small group have taken to each other spontaneously, the ensuing relationship will be more harmonious than anything you will see in a pair that was more or less arbitrarily combined for "rational" considerations. In parrots that bond by choice, problems in synchronizing mating cycles, incubating eggs, or raising young are practically unknown.

Unfortunately, it is a rare aviculturist who can assemble a small flock of parrots so that the birds can choose partners freely. As already mentioned, housing such a flock takes a lot of aviary space as well as money. Most parrot fanciers have no choice but to play matchmaker. But the increase in breeding successes since the introduction of endoscopy for sexing parrots justifies optimism and the hope that even arbitrarily matched birds can produce offspring with some predictability.

The Molting Cycle and How Temperature Affects It

As a rule, the breeding period is followed by the yearly molt. Soon after the young leave the nest or during the last few weeks when they are still fed by their parents, the adult birds change their plumage. (Eclectus parrots start molting during the incubating period.) The old feathers, many of them worn and tattered, are shed and replaced within 6–8 weeks by new feathers that restore the birds' full flying mobility and protect them from the cold.

The best time of year for parrots to mate and raise young in north central Europe is, of course, during the warm season. In other words, our birds ideally mate in the summer months and start molting immediately after, perhaps in September. Freshly imported parrots rarely conform to this schedule because their entire internal timetable has been disrupted by capture, isolation during the quarantine period, and geographic dislocation. These birds may molt unexpectedly or at the wrong season, so that producing and raising young is out of the question. Birds never enter the mating cycle during the molt. By regulating the birds' physical environment, however, we can influence these physiological processes so that the molt recurs predictably at a certain time of year, preferably between late August and October. Only if such a routine is established will birds raise a family after a winter rest.

The aviculturist can induce the molt in the fall by keeping the birds "cold." What is meant by this is that the parrots are kept in outdoor aviaries in the summer (with access to a shelter in bad weather) and remain in the shelter, where a steady temperature of about 50°F (10°C) is maintained, during the winter. Of course this presumes that an indoor-outdoor aviary is available.

Parrots that are not yet acclimated (see Getting Settled, page 25) have to be introduced to these conditions *slowly*. During their second summer they should gradually get used to spending all their time in the outdoor aviary. In bad weather and especially at night, they should be able to retreat to the enclosed shelter. Depending on the weather, the parrots should spend some time outdoors every day until late summer, but when the temperature drops below 59°F (15°C) they should stay in the shelter, which is kept at about 55–59°F (12–15°C). Under

63

Raising Parrots

these conditions the parrots can spend the entire winter in the shelter or birdhouse. On exceptionally nice fall and winter days they should be allowed a few hours in the open-air aviary. The following spring, the birds are again slowly introduced to spending all day in the open air. During their third winter they are treated as the year before, but the temperature in the shelter should be 5–9°F (2–5°C) lower than the previous winter. After a long enough acclimation phase, parrots will do very well in a shelter that is kept at about 50°F (10°C).

Keeping parrots relatively cold like this has the advantage that they do not have to undergo major temperature changes when they move back and forth between the outdoor aviary and the shelter. You can see how much smoother are these transitions than if the parrots were to spend the winter indoors at our customary inside temperatures of 68–72°F (20–22°C), move outdoors in May when the thermometer may well drop to 45 or 50°F (8–10°C), and back again in the fall. Temperature fluctuations of as much as 25°F (15°C) have a negative effect in the long run. Birds subjected to them several times a year not only fail to establish a regular physiological rhythm in captivity but are also prime candidates for respiratory diseases, which often lead to complications.

If parrots are kept as just described (after a carefully controlled acclimation period for freshly imported birds), their natural rhythm, which was disrupted by the hardships undergone during capture and shipment, has a chance to re-establish itself. After 2–4 years the parrots, regardless of the climatic conditions in their natural habitat,

will start their courtship and mating cycle in May or whenever the spring brings warmer weather. The molt will set in when the young become independent late in August or early September and will usually be concluded by the time winter arrives.

The Right Nesting Facilities

With a few exceptions, parrots are hole nesters. In the wild, most of them nest in natural tree holes, although some like rock crevices or caves and others dig holes in termite hills.

Large parrots living in captivity are not very particular about nest boxes and, if they are in breeding condition, accept almost any dark corner where they can sit on their eggs without being disturbed. I have read in avicultural magazines of parrots that nested between books on a bookshelf or in tin and plastic tubs. These should not be considered examples to be followed. The aviculturist should offer the birds nesting facilities that are suitable for parrots.

Nest Boxes
Pieces of hollow logs make good nest boxes for parrots and are sometimes available through pet stores (usually you have to order them specially) or directly from a manufacturer (look for addresses in avicultural magazines). Logs big enough for large parrots

Blue-fronted Amazon taking to the air. The wing markings of a species are displayed prominently in flight. ▷

64

are quite expensive and are not easy to make yourself. You would have to have access to fairly large logs (8–24 inches in diameter; 20–60 cm; see table on this page) and be able to handle a chain saw. You can use the chain saw to hollow out the log, but it takes some patience. Bore the saw straight down into the log, and make several cuts until the log is hollow. Then plug the ends with round slices of log about 2 inches (4–5 cm) thick. The top should be held in place by only one fairly long nail so that it can be swiveled to the side when you need to open and clean the box.

Make an entry hole in the upper third of the box. You can cut it out with a keyhole saw, which can also be used for cutting out a peephole 4 inches (10 cm) from the bottom. The peephole should be opened only when absolutely necessary to check if any eggs have been laid or if they have hatched. The hole can also be used to remove eggs for artificial incubation (see page 76) or to take out nestlings that have to be hand-raised (see page 76). Inside the nest box a few hardwood slats should be mounted below the entry hole to make it easier for the birds to climb out.

You can make perfectly adequate nest boxes from boards. Be sure to use solid wood, not pressboard or plyboard, which warps quickly when exposed to moisture.

The wood should not be painted or treated with any preservative but left in its natural state with no foreign smells. Parrots prefer nest boxes that no longer look or smell "new." Brightly or garishly colored boxes tend to be avoided by the parrots, even though, as mentioned earlier, parrots occasionally chose much more unlikely spots in which to nest.

Another possibility is to construct an imitation log box by covering a square box made of ordinary boards with bark or so-called slab wood available at some lumber yards.

Young parrots.
Above left: Rose-breasted cockatoo chicks, 16 and 18 days old. Above right: Young gray parrots, about 5 weeks old. Below left: Scarlet macaw chicks, 34 and 37 days old. Below right: A 6-week-old yellow-cheeked Amazon.

Dimensions of the Nest Box

Parrot Species	Height (in cm)	Inside diameter	Diameter of entry hole
Hyacinth, blue and gold, and other large macaws	150	40–60	15–20
Small macaws	80–100	30–35	10–12
Poicephalus parrots and caiques	60	20	8
Pionus parrots	80	25	10
Amazons, gray parrots, small cockatoos, and eclectus parrots	80–100	30–35	10–12
Moluccan, greater sulfur-crested, and umbrella-crested cockatoos	150	40–50	12–15

Raising Parrots

Bedding for the Nest

Since most parrots do not use nesting material, it is a good idea to cover the bottom of the nest box with a layer of wood shavings or soft, crumbly wood from the center of decaying trees. Some aviculturists use a mixture of peat and wood shavings, but peat has one drawback: It encourages the growth of mold, which can cause a fungus infection called aspergillosis (see page 45).

Suitable nest boxes for parrots. Left: Hollow log (available at pet stores). The peephole cut out of the side can be closed by sliding a metal pin through the small hoops on the cutout piece. Right: Homemade nest box. The cover and the observation door flip open.

I use almost exclusively crumbly wood, which can be found all year round in the woods. A 4-inch (10-cm) layer of this in the bottom of the box makes a nice bed for the eggs. With the weight of the sitting bird on top, the eggs form small depressions in the litter, where they rest securely without rolling around. The moisture in the decaying wood also forestalls hatching complications. If you use wood shavings, I suggest that you dampen them well before use or submerge the bottom of the nest box in water

for several hours for the wood to soak up water. This will later help the hatching go more smoothly, but of course you should not overdo the soaking. Standing water in the box and mold are bad for the eggs and the nestlings. One great advantage of a hollow log over a nest box built of boards is that it is easier to keep up the humidity in the former.

Supplementary Foods for the Breeding Period

If your parrots get a balanced and varied diet, it is not absolutely necessary to offer them a special soft food mixture for rearing baby birds. In many cases, however, especially when no sprouted seeds or animal proteins are supplied, introducing rearing food during the reproductive phase is advisable. Of course, as with any other unfamiliar food, the birds take a while to get used to it.

One rearing mixture that is easy to prepare at home consists of low-fat, dry cottage cheese; unflavored bread crumbs; hard-boiled egg yolk; and some calcium and vitamins. The mixture should be somewhat moist but still crumbly, and it should never — especially in the summer — be left in the aviary for more than 5–6 hours. It spoils easily and can then cause serious digestive problems.

Pet stores also carry perfectly adequate ready-mixed foods, sometimes labeled as rearing, egg, or soft-bill food. They generally come in the form of pellets fortified with various nutritional supplements and can be given to the birds either dry or slightly moistened.

Even though this food is labeled rearing food, you should not wait until there are nestlings to be reared before you offer it. Parrots often take a long time before they sample food they are not used to. Even when you first introduce sprouted seeds or grains — which are after all not too dissimilar from regular seeds — it may take days before the first bird decides to taste them. After that the partner, too, will start eating them.

You should get your parrots used to rearing food and whatever other supplements you want them to have well in advance so that there will be no nutritional gap when the young hatch. However, I have heard repeatedly from other aviculturists — and found out myself with one pair of birds — that in spite of all the keeper's efforts the parent birds sometimes refuse to take supplementary foods until the day of hatching. In my case the parent birds waited until they had to provide food for their young before they suddenly accepted the soft food they had spurned for weeks before. From then on they took it and fed it to their young until the nestlings left the nest and learned to eat seeds on their own.

The Incubation Period

Parrots living in the northern temperate zone usually get ready to breed at the end of April or in early May if they have molted in the previous fall (see The Molting Cycle and How Temperature Affects It, page 63).

Birds that have not yet established a regular molting cycle or that are kept at the same temperature summer and winter may enter breeding condition in any season. Cockatoos and eclectus parrots can breed all year round (except during molt) so that they may produce more than one clutch per year. Gray parrots and most South American parrots always breed at the same time of year and raise only one family annually.

What the Aviculturist Should Watch for
Various kinds of courtship behavior (see page 70) initiate the mating season and signal to the keeper that special care is now in order. Adjustments in housing (removing neighbors or aviary companions that might interfere) and in diet (rearing food) are called for, and nest boxes have to be supplied. A close eye should be kept on the birds' general state of health, for raising offspring puts great demands on the physical system. If your parrots are breeding for the first time, you should check to make sure that the hen has no problems laying the eggs (see Egg Binding, page 48), that the birds sit on the eggs, and that the eggs hatch and the parent birds feed the hatchlings. It takes a certain intuition and sensitivity to notice the subtle changes in behavior and to check at the right time. Whatever you do, don't give in to impatience and curiosity and peer into the nest box every few hours to see what is happening inside. If you do, you may scare the female, and in her fright to get away she may break the eggs, or she may refuse to return to the box, abandoning the eggs or baby birds.

Most parrots exhibit some changes in behavior several weeks before they produce eggs. Pairs that have accepted each other and are in breeding condition suddenly turn aggressive toward other birds in the colony or in neighboring aviaries. Any bird that intrudes into the pair's privacy is attacked

Raising Parrots

with loud screeching, fanned tail, spread wings, and narrowed pupils and, if necessary, pursued to the point of exhaustion. Even the keeper is not safe from attack, although the parrots may accept him or her and even be tame outside of mating season. The birds can turn into regular furies capable of inflicting painful wounds. For many years I only read about such incidents, but one day I experienced the anger of a parrot firsthand. I wanted to introduce a male to a female blue-fronted Amazon that had lived in my birdhouse for years and had always been rather timid in my presence. An endoscopic examination had revealed that the partner she had been sharing her quarters with was another female. I placed the male in the aviary with her in the morning. To my disappointment no friendly relations seemed to develop between the two, so I decide to separate them again at night. When I entered the aviary to catch the male, the female immediately flew at me in a rage, dug her claws into my shoulder, reduced my shirt and sweater to shreds within a few seconds , and tore five heavily bleeding gashes in my skin. I found myself completely unable at first to shake the bird off, something I would not have imagined possible before.

The Courtship Ritual

The courtship ritual of most of the parrots described in this book is not as spectacular as that of some other birds. The male is quite striking when he tries to impress the female by strutting up and down his favorite perch. He stands as tall as possible, neck feathers raised, tail spread, and shoulders squared (cockatoos with crest erect), displaying all his physical attributes to best advantage. This is done not only to impress the chosen female but also to appear larger and more threatening to potential rivals. Other typical behavior associated with courtship is partner feeding and mutual preening. Social or mutual preening can be observed all year round, but during courtship the birds engage in it much more often and intensively. Outside the mating season the primary purpose of mutual

During the courtship display, a male parrot often feeds his mate; this serves as a rehearsal for his later role of provider for the female and the nestlings.

preening is to get the parts of the body cleaned that are not easily accessible to the bird's own bill (head and rump), but during courtship mutual preening takes on added meaning: It expresses the birds' sense of belonging together. In situations of potential conflict, social preening (or scratching, as some aviculturists call it) enhances the bond between the pair and strengthens their resolve to defend their territory and nest.

Partner feeding can be observed frequently in parrots that are preparing to mate (except for cockatoos, which never exhibit this behavior). With a strange jerking and

Raising Parrots

pumping motion of the head and neck the male regurgitates some partially digested liquid food — sometimes called crop milk — from his crop and feeds it to the female, who assumes a posture similar to that of begging baby birds. Like mutual preening, partner feeding has two functions. It serves as practice for later when the male has to feed his mate and the baby bird for several weeks. When the nestlings are fed, the male brings the predigested food to the female, who passes it on to the babies. The male parent does not feed the young directly until they are about 3 weeks old. At that point the female starts leaving the nest box again to help provide food for the growing young. The second function of partner feeding is that, like mutual preening, it strengthens the bond between the mates.

A male blue-fronted Amazon demonstrating the courtship display. He is wooing his chosen female by raising the feathers on his nape and fanning out his tail.

The Mating

You can often tell that a female is ready to mate by the way she sits on the perch. She lies almost flat, trembling all over and extending her wings slightly, thus inviting the male. I have also observed this behavior in birds that had been caged without a partner for years.

Long before the eggs are due, the birds begin to show interest in the nest box. The dark entry hole seems to exert a magical attraction, and the birds begin to gnaw persistently on its rim. One or both birds spend hours at a time busying themselves with the nest box or sitting inside it. At this point they may mate several times a day. Weeks before, when the male tentatively approached the female, she had probably rebuffed him because she was not yet ready to mate.

Most large parrots mate on a perch. The male laboriously climbs onto the female (he doens't fly on top of her as some other birds do), grips the feathers of her flanks with his claws, and tries, moving rhythmically, to bring his cloaca — the cavity into which the sexual organs of both sexes open — in contact with hers so that fertilization will occur. During this act of "stepping on" the female, as some aviculturists call it, he maintains his balance by holding on to her nape feathers with his bill. Male parrots native to the New World — South and Central America — place only one foot on the female's back and hold on to the perch with the other. Macaws, and sometimes Amazons, occasionally mate while sitting next to each other on the perch, raising their tails up in the air and pushing their cloacas against each other. In cockatoos it is usually the female that initiates the mating.

Raising Parrots

Females in a mating mood invite males by lying flat on the perch, trembling all over, and partially unfolding their wings. (The drawing depicts a Senegal parrot.)

By assuming the typical mating posture (described on page 71), she arouses the male and thus determines when copulation takes place.

Laying the Eggs

Many African parrots like sleeping in their nest boxes even when they are not breeding. In the other species, which generally ignore the box when they are not in breeding condition, it is much easier to tell when they are about to use the box for raising a family. If you see the female spending time inside it, even sleeping there at night, this is a sign that she is getting ready to lay her eggs. Large and sometimes mushy piles of droppings on the aviary floor indicate that the female is leaving the nest as little as possible.

Many parrots living in captivity lay their eggs in May or June; cockatoos and eclectus parrots sometimes lay earlier. The favorite times of day for egg laying are the early morning and the late afternoon.

A clutch usually consists of two or three, more rarely four or five eggs, which are laid at intervals of 2 days. Sometimes eggs follow each other after only 36 hours, and sometimes the intervals may be as much as 72 hours. Parrots' eggs are white like the eggs of all other birds that nest in cavities where color is not necessary for camouflage. They are oval, slightly pointed, and have a smooth, often shiny surface.

The eggs of the parrots described in this book weigh between 3.3 to 6.7 % of the adult bird's weight. Thus the egg of a blue and gold macaw weighs about 33 g; of a Moluccan cockatoo, about 30 g; of an eclectus parrot, about 22 g; of a gray parrot, about 21 g; of a blue-fronted Amazon, about 18 g; of a lesser sulfur-crested cockatoo, about 17 g; and of a Senegal parrot, about 9 g.

The sizes of the eggs are given in the following table.

Size of Eggs

Moluccan cockatoo	50.0 × 33.4 mm
Lesser sulfur-crested cockatoo	41.2 × 27.1 mm
Umbrella-crested cockatoo	40.8 × 30.8 mm
Eclectus parrot	40.2 × 31.0 mm
Blue and gold macaw	46.4 × 35.9 mm
Severe macaw	38.4 × 30.4 mm
Noble macaw	32.8 × 26.9 mm
Gray parrot	39.4 × 31.0 mm
Blue-fronted Amazon	38.1 × 29.6 mm
Mealy Amazon	37.7 × 29.0 mm
Spectacled Amazon	30.2 × 22.7 mm
Red-vented parrot	33.8 × 25.6 mm
Brown parrot	27.0 × 24.0 mm

Raising Parrots

Incubation and Hatching

The female begins to sit on the nest after laying the second egg. In cockatoos, the male and the female take turns sitting on the eggs, but this is an exception. In the other species the female incubates the eggs almost exclusively by herself. This explains why "partner feeding" is not part of the courtship ritual with cockatoos. Unlike African and South American parrots, in which the female sits on the eggs all the time and is therefore dependent on her mate for food, cockatoos have no need for this divison of roles. Since both parents take turns sitting, each has time off the nest when each bird can find food for itself and later for the young. It would seem, then, that nature omitted partner feeding in the courtship ritual of cockatoos

Length of Incubation (Days)

Hyacinth macaw	28–30
Blue and gold macaw	25
Scarlet and green-winged macaws	25–28
Smaller macaws	24–27
Amazons	28
Pionus parrots	28
Caiques	25–28
Moluccan cockatoo	30
Umbrella-crested cockatoo	28
Lesser sulfur-crested cockatoo	22–24
Rose-breasted cockatoo	22–24
Eclectus parrots	28
Gray parrots	30
Long-winged parrots	22–25

because this particular behavior is not needed later for the survival of the female and the baby birds.

Incubation ends with the hatching of the young and is followed by the rearing period. Baby parrots (of the species mentioned in this book) hatch after an incubation period of approximately 21–30 days.

At the same intervals at which the eggs were laid, that is, about every 48 hours, the baby birds hatch one by one. Parrots are nidiculous birds, which means that the nestlings take a long time to develop independence and need their parents' guidance for quite a long time even after leaving the nest.

Problems During Incubation

Incubation does not always go smoothly and automatically result in baby birds. I have heard aviculturist friends say — and it has happened to me, too, more often than I would like — that "something went wrong" and the eggs did not hatch. Some possible reasons for failure are as follows.

• Two newly matched parrots had not yet taken a liking to each other (and perhaps never will), so that no mating took place. In such a situation eggs are laid and conscientiously incubated by the female even though they are infertile. If this happens, the eggs should be removed after the normal incubation period (see table on this page). The female then often proceeds to lay a second clutch even if she belongs to a species that ordinarily raises only one brood per year.

• If the parent bird left the nest for too long a time, the eggs may have gotten too cold, causing the death of the embryos. The reason the bird left the eggs unattended is not always easy to determine, but one thing that is certain is that if the female is disturbed too often she is likely to respond by leaving the nest.

• It happens not infrequently that fully developed parrot chicks die inside the egg shortly before hatching. They die because they are not able to break out of the shell. The reason usually is that the air was too dry in the nest box, so that the shells became too hard and brittle for the fully mature chick to crack them. You can prevent this disappointing outcome by moistening the nesting material before the eggs are laid and by spraying the outside of the nest box with water every so often during the incubation period. Of course you should not overdo this by keeping the box constantly wet, let alone dripping with water, because far from aiding the hatching process, the excess moisture may well kill the embryos.

The Development and Rearing of the Young

Baby parrots usually emerge from the egg completely naked or only sparsely covered with light down. For the first few hours they are unable to sit up, and their eyes are closed. Since the eggs hatch in the order in which they were laid, there are usually nestlings of different ages in the same nest. In many cases only the bigger ones survive because the younger ones, being smaller and weaker, cannot assert themselves forcefully enough to get fed and eventually die. This seems to happen quite often with cockatoos. If the caretaker does not interfere, only a single

A female bare-eyed cockatoo feeding her chick. While being fed, the chick makes cheeping sounds and lightly flaps its wings.

nestling may survive and the younger siblings are pushed aside at feeding times and starve to death. In nature, the chicks that hatch second and third apparently serve merely as backups in case the oldest does not survive for some reason.

The aviculturist can step in by giving the birds additional, suitable soft food or by taking the smaller nestlings out of the nest and hand-rearing them (see page 76).

The baby parrots are soon able to rise up and beg for food. The mother bird responds by grasping the nestling's bill with hers at a right angle and regurgitating some food, or crop milk, that she feeds to the nestling. This routine will be re-enacted many times until the young reach independence.

From about the third week on, the male, whose task thus far was restricted to supply-

Raising Parrots

A scarlet macaw chick at various stages of development.

8 days: The eyes are still shut and will not open until the tenth or twelfth day. The chick weighs barely 4 ounces (100 g).

32 days: The pin feathers on the wings, the tail, and the head are pushing through.

35 days: The chick now weighs almost 1½ pounds (700 g.)

38 days: The feathers are now clearly visible on the head, wings, and tail. The chick now weighs almost 28 ounces (800 g.)

ing the female with food, takes an active part in the feeding of the young, which gradually begin to look like parrots. The eyes open in the third or fourth week, depending on the species, and by the end of the fourth week the first thin down has given way to a thick, gray down coat. About a week later the first pinfeathers break through, and by the sixth week, red, blue, yellow, or white areas, depending on the particular markings of the species, are recognizable. The first real plumage is fully grown in at about 8 or 10 weeks, which is also when the young birds first start leaving the nest box for short spells. At night they still return to sleep there.

Length of the Nestling Period (Days)

Large macaws	80–100
Small macaws	60–70
Amazons	About 70
Pionus parrots and caiques	60–70
Umbrella-crested and Moluccan cockatoos	80–90
Small cockatoos	60–70
Eclectus and gray parrots	About 75
Poicephalus parrots	45–60

Even after leaving the nest, the fledglings still need their parents' care. At this point it is primarily the male that looks after them while the mother bird often ignores her offspring's begging or actively fends them off. Young parrots learn to find their own food only slowly. At first they live primarily on soft food and fruit, and it takes them some time to succeed in extricating seeds from the shell.

Raising Parrots

Artificial Incubation and Hand-Raising Young Parrots

Parrots occasionally abandon their eggs or neglect to feed their nestlings (or feed only one chick, as in the case of cockatoos; see page 95). Abandoned eggs, if they are discovered soon enough, before the embryos die, can be kept warm in an incubator until the chicks are ready to hatch. The best incubation temperature is about 101°F (38.5°C), with a slight increase to about 104°F (40°C) toward the end. The humidity should be about 70–80%.

The eggs should be turned several times a day and allowed to cool slightly for about 10 minutes once or twice a day. Most commercially sold incubators automatically turn and air the eggs. Cockatoo eggs do not need to be cooled because under natural conditions both parents take turns brooding and one is always sitting on the eggs.

Artificially incubated eggs hatch 1 to 2 days earlier than a clutch brooded by the parent birds. The newly hatched parrots should be placed in a dark container, such as a plastic bucket that is loosely covered so that air can circulate, and located near an even heat source (the temperature should be kept around 90°F/32°C). You can use soft paper tissue as bedding for the nestlings at first, changing it as needed several times a day. Later, fine wood shavings can be used to line the artificial nest.

Feeding Hand-Raised Nestlings

Trying to feed newly hatched parrot babies is not easy because under normal circumstances the parent birds feed their offspring from the crop, grasping the young bird's bill with their own and transferring the crop milk to the nestling's stomach with jerking motions. If you hand-rear baby parrots you have to imitate this method. After each mouthful you have to take the bird's bill between your thumb and index finger and move it up and down.

The gruel for the nestlings can be made up of oatmeal with some glucose added or of softened zwieback or baby cereal with a little bit of hard-boiled egg yolk. Moisten whatever you use with some lukewarm water.

Add a few drops of vitamin supplement and some calcium to this gruel every second or third day. To avoid giving an overdose (especially of vitamins A and D), it is best to use a vitamin supplement of low dosage, such as those sold at pet stores for small caged birds.

Baby parrots can live on the yolk stored in the egg for about 10–15 hours before they have to be fed for the first time. When you do feed them, use a disposable plastic hypodermic syringe, available at drugstores. To keep from injuring the tender throat, replace the needle with a thin rubber tube about 2 inches long (like the ones used in bicycle tire valves). Fill the syringe with slightly warmed food, and then push several small portions into the bill in quick succession, thus trying to induce the bird to swallow. Another and much less time-consuming method is to pump the food directly into the crop. In young, still nearly naked nestlings you can see quite clearly through the thin skin how the food accumulates inside the crop. Feed just enough to barely fill the crop so that it is still soft to the touch.

Raising Parrots

In the beginning the food has to be quite liquid and at about wrist temperature. For the first 3–4 weeks, the nestlings have to be fed regularly ever 2 hours during the day (from 6 a.m. to 10 p.m.; not during the night). As they grow older, the time between feedings is increased to 3 and then 4 hours. After 4 weeks the feeding method changes. Then you try to get the birds to eat from a spoon. The food given can be more solid and is supplemented with grated fruit, finely chopped hard-boiled egg, and commercial rearing food. You also start adding ground grain, gradually increasing the amount. Toward the end of the nestling period the number of meals is reduced to three a day and a shallow bowl of sprouted seeds is offered for snacks. It won't be long before the birds can handle ordinary birdseed.

A hand-raised parrot that never had any contact with its parents will completely adopt its human caretaker and develop into an extremely tame and playful indoor bird that will soon try to imitate human speech. However, because it does not know how other birds of its own species look and behave, it will probably not be able to mate later. It more or less looks on its caretaker as one of its own kind, and trying to integrate the bird into a community of other parrots will always be problematic, even though there are isolated cases of hand-raised parrots successfully reproducing.

Hybrid Offspring

Hybrid offspring are the result of a successful mating between two birds of different species or races. As a rule, these matings are between members of the same genus (blue and gold and green-winged macaws, or blue-fronted and orange-winged Amazons, or lesser sulfur-crested and umbrella-crested cockatoos) or between two races of the same species (yellow-cheeked and Lesson's Amazons). Successful matings between representatives of two different genera are much rarer and generally occur only if there is a close relationship between them. Examples are offspring from a hyacinth macaw (genus *Anodorhynchus*) and a blue and gold macaw (genus *Ara*) or from a lesser sulfur-crested cockatoo (genus *Cacatua*) and a rose-breasted cockatoo (genus *Eolophus*).

One recent example shows that even more distantly related parrots can produce viable offspring. In 1984, the crossing of a female Illiger's macaw and a male black-headed caique in the Duisberg Zoo produced four healthy young parrots. Like most hybrids, they exhibited the shapes and markings of both parents.

In nature, matings between animals belonging to different species — and consequently the production of hybrid offspring — are prevented by various factors, such as nonsynchronous mating seasons, differences in courtship ritual, or geographic barriers, like mountain ranges, that isolate different species from each other.

Still, hybrids or mongrels, as they are sometimes called, do occur in nature in areas where the ranges of two species meet and overlap. This phenomenon is scientifically documented, for instance in the border area between Brazil and Peru, where white-bellied and black-headed caiques occupy adjacent ranges and overlap because no river

Raising Parrots

divides their territories. Hybrid parrots with characteristics of both species have been observed there. (In the rest of these parrots' huge area of distribution, the Amazon River serves as a boundary that keeps the two species apart.)

Hybrid parrots turn up with some frequency among captive birds. When not enough or only unsatisfactory partners of the right species are available, birds of different species readily pair up, and the resulting relationship may be just as harmonious as that between a pair of similar birds. In many zoos where Amazons and macaws are kept together in large community aviaries, such "mixed marriages" are quite routine although they do not always produce offspring. In America, crossings between different macaws, especially between the blue and gold *(Ara ararauna)* and the scarlet macaw *(A. macao)*, are apparently so common that their offspring have been given a name of their own, namely, the Catalina macaw.

Zoologists object on principle to the production of hybrids because, as has happened in many animal species in the past, it may hasten the extinction of some species in their original forms if the wild populations are already significantly decimated. It is true that hybrids generally cannot produce offspring of their own so that further change in the original gene composition is precluded, but there are a number of species in which the original form no longer survives — at least in our aviaries — because of human manipulation in attempts to breed birds for certain characteristics. Examples are the various Australian rosellas and red-fronted parakeets *(Cyanoramphus novaezelandiae)* of New Zealand whose different races have been arbitrarily crossed so often that probably not a single untampered specimen survives in captivity. A similar situation exists with African lovebirds. The masked, Fischer's, Nyasa, and black-cheeked lovebirds have been so manipulated and deformed by fanciers' breeding ambitions that it is often impossible to tell to which species or subspecies a particular bird should be assigned. All aviculturists should make it a point to get mates of the same species or race for their single parrots so that the birds can reproduce as they would in nature, namely, with birds of their own kind.

Bird Shows

In many places bird shows are held every year between September and December. Successful breeders can exhibit the young birds hatched in the course of the year and get a chance to compare them with those of other breeders. These events may be organized by local bird societies or groups of fanciers, by larger regional or national groups, or by international organizations. (You will find more information on parrot societies on page 141).

All the birds raised in captivity are presented in standard cages, organized by species and groups or color variants, to judges who compare the birds and evaluate them according to a number of criteria. The winning bird in each category — or rather the bird's owner — receives a trophy that will later serve as proof of the honor received at the exhibition.

Raising Parrots

Although by far the greatest number of exhibited birds are finches, canaries, rosellas, budgerigars, and lovebirds, more and more parrots are shown, too, every year. We take this as a sign that breeding efforts with large parrots are becoming more frequent, which is presumably due at least in part to the ceaseless work and exchange of information in which the exhibiting groups and associations engage.

Threatening stance. With open beak and often with spread wings, each parrot tries to convey to the other that it had better withdraw.

Does It Make Sense to Exhibit Parrots?

If exhibiting one's birds becomes an end in itself and if, as I have seen among many aviculturists, the chase after trophies becomes the primary motive for breeding parrots, it is perhaps time to re-examine one's motives for having and breeding parrots.

It also seems questionable to me in general whether large parrots are suitable for exhibiting at all. After all, these parrots will probably never be bred on a sufficiently large scale for such criteria as those used in normal selective breeding of birds like canaries and budgerigars to be applied. A veterinarian once defined "breeding" — as the term is traditionally applied to domestic animals — as "the planned reproduction of an animal species, controlled by humans with the aim of stabilizing or enhancing certain characteristics or combining them in new ways to achieve specific goals in the next generation." This definition can be applied without hesitation to most of the birds seen at bird shows, but it is meaningless, and probably always will be, in connection with the large parrots discussed in this book. The idea of a show to compare one's own breeding results with those of others seems to me almost grotesque in connection with large parrots because at present we are not able to breed enough parrots to ensure the survival of all the species, let alone to start thinking of "selective" breeding for certain traits.

In my opinion there are other reasons as well for thinking twice before showing parrots at exhibitions.

Exhibitions Are a Trial for the Parrots

Getting ready to go to a bird exhibition means the following for the parrots involved:
• Being torn out of their social community (temporary separation from other birds of the same species and especially from the mate)

Raising Parrots

- Having to get used to a small exhibition cage
- Daily training to learn the proper sitting posture required by the exhibition guidelines
- Washing and grooming of the plumage (involving repeated capture and handling of the birds)

When the date of the show arrives, this is what is in store for the parrots:

- A trip to the exhibition location
- Adjustment to different temperatures from those to which the birds are accustomed at home
- Bad air in the exhibition halls, often poisoned by cigarette smoke
- The possibility of catching a disease from other birds, always a real danger even though the guidelines of many organizations require a veterinarian's certificate of health for all birds entering shows.
- Being disturbed continually by thousands of exhibition visitors, many of whom — from what I have seen — cannot refrain from trying to touch the birds through the bars or trying to get the bird's attention by rattling the cage.

It seems to me that any one of these points might dissuade a lover of parrots from getting involved in bird exhibitions. The cumulative impact of all these negative experiences on parrots seems to me cause for seriously questioning the concept and justification of these events and for reconsidering our own moral responsibility toward the birds in our care.

Whatever your feelings about bird shows may be, I urge you to visit one sometime and look at the parrots there with the eyes of an objective observer. Perhaps you will understand what I mean when you see the plight of umbrella-crested and rose-crested cockatoos and even large macaws cramped into cages that are far too small to allow even the most basic of their occupants' needs.

To me, neither the chance to compare birds (meaningless, as I have already argued), nor the desire on the part of the exhibitor to have a larger audience appreciate his or her birds, nor the hope of collecting a sheaf of trophies justifies putting the birds through days of upheaval and discomfort.

Parrot Biology

The Scientific Classification of Parrots

Parrots make up the order of Psittaciformes (parrots and allies), which most zoologists subdivide into three families. Of the approximately 320–330 different parrot species known, 18 belong to the Cacatuidae family (cockatoos, including the cockatiel); about 55 make up the Loriidai family (lories and lorikeets); and the rest, some 250 species, are assigned to the Psittacidae family (all other parrots). The closest relatives of the parrots are probably the woodpeckers, the cuckoos, the pigeons, and the owls, birds that have anatomic, morphological, physiological, and ethological traits in common with parrots.

Distinguishing Characteristics of Parrots

Unlike many other kinds of birds that are hard to identify, parrots are easy to recognize even by people who don't know anything about birds. Parrots vary greatly in size (from 4 inches, 10 cm, in the case of the pygmy parrots — found in New Guinea and the Solomon Islands — to the 40 inches or so, 100 cm, of a hyacinth macaw), as well as in color, but their other characteristic traits are so striking that parrots are rarely confused with other birds.

One typical characteristic of all large parrots is their short, stubby body with a relatively short neck and big head. With the exception of the macaws, all the parrots described in this book (see page 95) have short, rounded tails made up of twelve feathers. Cockatoos also have a more or less pronounced crest that generally differs in color from the rest of the body and can be raised when the birds are in a state of agitation or fright or are ready to attack or defend themselves.

An especially striking feature of all parrots is their powerful, hooked, and very mobile beak, which serves them as a kind of "third foot" in climbing.

The feet are another distinctive feature. The four strong toes, equipped with claws, are arranged differently from those of most other birds in that two toes are directed forward and two point backward. Parrots share this toe arrangement, the technical name for which is *zygodactyl*, with woodpeckers and cuckoos. These feet not only make excellent tools for climbing but they are also used for holding on to large chunks of food.

The predominant color of parrots is green, but there are some species that are almost uniformly white or black (most cockatoos, for instance), and some have markings of different colors (red, yellow, and blue, as well as other shades).

Sensory Organs and Capacities

Like most other birds, parrots have excellent powers of sight. Their eyes, which function very much like a zoom lens in a camera, are undoubtedly their most important sensory organ, and parrots can very accurately identify objects both close up and at a considerable distance. Experiments have shown that parrots are also able to distinguish dif-

Parrot Biology

ferent colors, and it is well-known that they can spot ripened farm products (such as grains and fruits) from great heights and will always select a ripened fruit over a green one when there is a choice. The vision of parrots is monocular, which means that the two eyes function independently of each other. The field of vision of parrots is apparently quite small, about 6–10°.

The sense of hearing is also well developed in parrots even though they lack external ears. Evidence from experiments suggests that they perceive a wide range of frequencies.

We are still largely in the dark about how well parrots can smell and taste, but it seems clear that these two senses are less well developed than in mammals. There is, however, speculation that various parrots can actually taste foods farther along the digestive tract, such as the region at the base of the tongue or even beyond this point. One thing we do know is that parrots, especially those that eat fruit, can tell which morsels are sweeter than others and consequently either refuse or only reluctantly eat some food while clearly relishing the sweet parts.

The Natural Distribution of Parrots

Parrots live on all the continents except Europe and the polar regions. Ornithologists believe that they originated in northern Australia and New Guinea, where the most typical and apparently oldest parrots are still found. From this place of evolutionary origin, parrots slowly spread over thousands of years to other parts of the earth, primarily the tropical and subtropical areas. The present range of distribution is divided into the following geographic zones.

The Pacific distribution: Australia, New Zealand, New Guinea, parts of Indonesia (Lesser Sunda and Moluccan islands, the Philippines, and Borneo), and numerous islands and archipelagos northeast of Australia (the Solomons, Fiji, and New Caledonia)

The Afro-Asian distribution: Africa, the Malagasy Republic (formerly the Island of Madagascar), Saudi Arabia, Iran, Pakistan, India, Indochina (Burma, Thailand, Laos, Vietnam, and Cambodia), the Malay Peninsula, the Indonesian islands (Sumatra and Java), and parts of Borneo

The South American distribution: South and Central America, the Caribbean Islands (Cuba, Jamaica, Hispaniola, Puerto Rico, the Bahamas, the Virgin Islands, and the Antilles), and the extreme south of North America

Fossil finds indicate that at one point parrots also inhabited parts of Europe. Parrots once lived south of the Alps in Spain and southern France.

North America, too, had its native parrot whose range extended about as far north as the Canadian border. The Carolina parakeet, once plentiful and slaughtered as a pest, barely survived into the twentieth century and died out just a few decades ago.

Australian rose-breasted cockatoos drink without alight- ▷ ing. Above: The cockatoo approaches the water and lowers its beak. Below: The beak is dipped in the water, and the bird quickly takes off again. This sensational series of shots was taken by the animal photographers Arendt and Schweiger.

Parrot Biology

The Natural Habitat of Parrots

Parrots live in very varied climatic zones and among different vegetation. Most of them come from tropical areas. The tropics, which extend to all continents except Europe and Antarctica, include not only tropical forests but also savannas, steppes, and semideserts.

Tropical forests, whether in Brazil, Indonesia, or central Africa, have constant warm temperatures around 82–86°F (28–30°C), which barely drop below 68°F (20°C) at night. The humidity is around 70–80% and almost reaches saturation in the early morning hours. Because of the geographic location of the rain forests (most of them are close to the equator), 12-hour days and nights are constant all year round.

The typical "jungle" vegetation is the result of high levels of precipitation, warm temperatures, and soils that encourage a lush and varied plant life. This rich vegetation offers parrots plenty of food year round so that they are able to reproduce any time of year. These parrots have no need for great flying skills because they do not have to range far in search of food and water.

The annual precipitation in savanna climates is at least 20 inches (500 mm), which is enough to permit brushy vegetation about 5 or 6 feet high with occasional groups of trees. The rainy seasons take up about 6–9 months of the year. Temperatures rise as high as 104°F (40°C) during the day but may drop as low as 50–59°F (10–15°C) during the night.

In the steppes the precipitation, which amounts to between 12 and 20 inches (300–500 mm) annually, all comes within 2–4 months. Vegetation is limited to grass varying in height from knee-high to chest-high, some shrubs or cacti, and moderately high trees, which lose their foliage during the long dry seasons. The annual average temperatures vary considerably.

Parrots that live in regions in which the entire rainfall is concentrated in a few months have to adjust their life functions to the givens of their environment and the rhythm of the annual weather cycle. Since steppes and savannas offer less protection than rain forests, parrots have to adopt a coloring that helps camouflage them, and they have to be better fliers. Flying skills are essential not only for quick escape from predators but also for finding and reaching watering places that are far away. Parrots living in savanna and steppe climates reproduce when food is most plentiful, that is, when the rains give rise to a short season of opulent vegetation.

Some parrots live in semiarid and arid regions, and a few species can even be found in subalpine and alpine zones.

Every kind of environment has its own climatic character and imposes special adaptive mechanisms on the creatures living there, mechanisms that have been formed gradually over the course of evolutionary history.

◄ Australian parrots in their natural habitat. Above: A mixed flock of rose-breasted and bare-eyed cockatoos. Below left: Bare-eyed cockatoo on the point of taking to the air. Below right: A pair of rose-breasted cockatoos investigating a nesting cavity.

Parrot Biology

Parrots Living in the Wild

The overwhelming majority of parrots are gregarious creatures that live together in families, small groups, or larger flocks all year round. Parrots living in tropical forests near the equator, where there is always plenty of food available, are likely to gather together in large flocks, often composed of several hundred birds, to go about the business of daily life together. Starting from a centrally located sleeping area, to which all the members of the flock return every evening, the birds go off in search of food. In such a flock there are almost always some individuals that act as watch birds and break into loud screeching when a predator appears or anything unusual happens, causing their foraging companions to fly up into the air.

In areas where food is scarcer at certain times of year, the groups of parrots encountered together are much smaller, seldom comprising more than twenty birds.

Young parrots don't relinquish their community life until they reach sexual maturity, when they form pairs and go off in search of a suitable nesting site. The behavior of parrots living in captivity suggests that the parrots of many species are monogamous, living together with the same mate for many years and raising their young together. If one partner dies or gets sick, the "widowed" bird will go in search of a new mate after a certain "mourning period."

Nesting Places

Most parrots use deep holes in trees for nesting, preferably trees that are tall and have an entry hole just large enough for the adult parrot to be able to slip through. They favor holes that result from natural causes, enlarging them if necessary with their efficient beaks. The wood chips generated by enlarging the hole are dropped inside the cavity and serve as bedding for the eggs the female later lays without making a regular nest out of other nesting materials. Some smaller members of the parrot family like to take over nesting cavities abandoned by woodpeckers. Apart from holes in trees, some parrots also use rock crannies for nesting, and some use their bills to dig holes in termite hills. A few species lay their eggs on the ground, well hidden in tall grass or among bushes. Monk parrots are unique in building huge communal nests from branches. The nests have several chambers for a number of families, including their young.

Many parrot couples breed in the same place year after year. In some areas of Central and South America, parrots have been breeding in certain trees for so long that the Indios living there have claimed ownership of these trees for their families and pass it on from generation to generation.

Incubation and Rearing the Young

A clutch of parrot eggs consists of two to five eggs, depending on the species, and is usually brooded by the female only. In some cockatoo species, however, the male takes turns sitting on the eggs during the day.

The female starts sitting on the eggs after laying the second egg, or sometimes later, so that the eggs do not all hatch at the same time but at the intervals at which they were laid. Thus a nest might contain a newly hatched chick along with others that are 2, 4, and 6 days old.

Parrot Biology

During the first few days after the hatching, the male parent procures all the food for both the mother bird and the nestlings. Then, after a while, the hen begins leaving the nest chamber to help find food for her brood.

At the end of the breeding cycle, when the young have left the nest, the parrot families usually gather together again in flocks in which the youngsters are taught all the essentials for survival. They learn to function and assert their place in a group of birds; they encounter predators and find out how to defend themselves against them; and they gain experience in searching for food.

Until they reach sexual maturity, which happens between the third and fifth year depending on the species, young parrots seem to stay together and form a kind of "youth group." Within this group, pairs of birds often make friends and enter a kind of "betrothal" in anticipation of the new cycle of reproduction they will start when they reach the proper age.

The Behavior of Parrots

In recent years ethologists have been giving more attention to parrots. Growing knowledge about more and more parrot species has resulted in quite a few books and scientific articles on individual parrots. In addition, we have a number of published reports from parrot fanciers and aviculturists. In fact, there is so much available information that it would be an unwieldy task to try to describe in any detail the behavior of every species, including the similarities and especially the differences between them. The general patterns of behavior common to all parrots that I present in this chapter, however, will supply the parrot fancier with enough basic knowledge to interpret his or her own observations correctly and to encourge paying attention to the "fine points" in the birds' behavior.

Nonsocial Behavior

Nonsocial behavior includes actions that essentially do not involve other birds. Some of these are locomotion, eating and drinking habits, and comfort behavior (grooming that the birds do without the help of others).

Locomotion
Depending on their habitat, some parrots rely more on flying and others more on climbing to get from place to place. Jungle dwellers among the Amazons, for instance, are expert climbers but poor fliers. In dense forests it is neither necessary nor useful to fly great distances in search of food, nesting sites, or sleeping places. For many members of the cockatoo subfamily and of the genus *Poicephalus*, however, long-distance flying is essential to survival; the steppes are an inhospitable environment where food, water, and good sleeping places are often a long way from each other.

Parrots living in cages, of course, have no opportunity to fly. They have to make do with climbing and doing acrobatics on the walls or hanging from the top of their cage and with hopping from perch to perch. The need for exercise is so great for all parrots — whether they are climbers or flyers — that life in a cage cannot possibly satisfy it. Caged birds should be offered a chance to fly freely in a room or to spend as much time as possible on a climbing tree.

In an aviary, smaller parrots fly quite a lot, whereas larger ones, regardless of their flying ability, often choose to get from one place to another by climbing since the short distance would permit only a few flaps of the wings anyway. Cockatoos also hop sometimes; they can leap a considerable distance from one perch to another with amazing ease.

Food Intake
Most parrots pick single seeds out of a food dish and shell them then and there, pressing them one at a time against the corrugations in the upper mandible with the tongue and removing the hull with the tip of the beak. A green-winged macaw, whose food dish was on the floor of his large, tall cage, invented his own variation. I saw him climb down the cage bars to the bottom, fill his lower mandible with sunflower seeds from the cup, and then climb back up on his perch, where he proceeded to eat them one after the other.

The Behavior of Parrots

This unusual behavior no doubt grew out of the discomfort the bird felt on the cage floor. In order not to have to descend from his safe perch for every seed, he had hit on this method of picking up a number of seeds and storing them in his beak.

Parrots shell all the seeds they eat. Each seed is pushed with the tongue against the ridges in the upper mandible and the shell removed with the tip of the beak.

Larger chunks of food, such as nuts, sections of fruit, and rosehips, are picked up with the bill but then usually held down with one food (see illustration on page 89) and eaten piece by piece or sometimes just picked apart. Parrots use their feet like hands to grasp food or other objects or to scratch themselves with (see page 6).

The drinking habits of parrots vary considerably. Some dip the beak in the water, then raise the head, lick the water off the roof of the mouth with the tongue, and swallow it. Other parrots toss their heads back while swallowing, and still others suck up the water, keeping their heads lowered to the water dish.

Comfort Behavior

The term "comfort behavior" is used for all activities connected with hygiene in the widest sense of the word.

Preening: Parrots go over their entire plumage thoroughly several times a day. The feathers of the various parts of the body are pulled through the bill one by one and thus cleaned. The care of the large wing and tail feathers is especially thorough. Any parrot owner should take the time now and then to watch how deftly the parrots twist their heads this way and that to reach the plumage everywhere. Except for the head, nape, and throat, all parts of the body are accessible to the bill. Even very long tail feathers (like those of the macaws) are pulled through the bill for their entire length.

Shaking: After each preening session, as well as after sleeping or napping, the feathers are rearranged in their proper order. To accomplish this the parrot raises all its feathers as high as it can and then, after a vigorous shake, lays them down smoothly again.

Scratching: Like most birds, parrots clean the feathers on the head by scratching. Large parrots use a gesture similar to that used to hold up food to eat. They raise one foot to the head in front of the wing and quickly scratch several times, often with the nail of the longest toe. The scratching motion is almost too fast for the eye to follow. For all parts of the head to be reached it has to be twisted and rotated to various positions. If a parrot scratches itself all the time, however, and also picks at the feathers on other parts of the body, it may be infested with parasites (see Ectoparasites, page 43).

The Behavior of Parrots

Beak care: To remove dirt and bits of food from the beak, parrots rub the upper mandible against something solid, usually a perch. Both sides are rubbed alternately several times. If some food that is sticking to the bill refuses to come off after several tries, most parrots resort to the foot, using a motion similar to scratching.

Parrots sharpen their bills and try to keep them worn down properly by gnawing on wood and by gnashing together the upper and lower mandible. This gnashing, which is usually done when the birds are resting, makes a cracking noise that is clearly audible.

Foot care: Parrots use their bills and their extremely mobile tongues to remove dirt and bits of hard skin from the feet. The foot is raised up to the bill for this purpose.

Bathing: Generally, large parrots cannot take baths in a cage. Some of them dip their heads into the water dish several times to get at least part of themselves wet. A parrot living in a cage should get a shower at least once a week, either from a hand-held shower head in the bathtub or from a plant mister. Most parrots quickly learn to appreciate a shower because it helps them get rid of feather dust. They show their enjoyment by raising their feathers, spreading their tails, and turning around on their perch so that the longed-for moisture can reach them from all angles. Make sure, though, that the water is not ice-cold, and schedule the bath for the morning so that the birds will have plenty of time to dry thoroughly before bedtime. Birds living in an aviary can be given a large, shallow, and stable bathing basin (see illustration on page 24). Many parrots will make use of such a basin often and with pleasure after a short period of getting used to this unfamiliar object. Very few parrots actually step into the water. They perch on the edge of the basin and start by dipping the beak in while shaking the head and sneezing. Then they plunge in the head, neck, and upper body several times in quick succession, with feathers standing up.

Of course you can spray or shower aviary parrots just as you do parrots in a cage. One practical method is to install a permanent sprinkling system in every aviary and activate it once every day during summer months. Or you can simply use an ordinary garden hose with a nozzle that can produce a fine spray. The birds adjust quickly to this daily summer shower. To the human observer it looks as though they greeted it with a "bath dance"; with visible pleasure they raise their feathers, slightly lift their wings, and, in order to expose as much of the plumage as possible to the water, beat their wings and twist and turn while the shower lasts. Cockatoos have one more way to express their enjoyment of the bath: They raise their crests to impressive heights. The bath is usually followed by an extended grooming session.

Stretching: Movements associated with metabolic processes, especially those that have to do with oxygen exchange (stretching and yawning, for example), are also considered part of comfort behavior. Birds stretch most often after resting. At first both wings are slightly spread across the back; they are just barely lifted, not fully extended. Then first one wing and then the other is stretched out. The feathers of one wing are spread wide at the same time that the leg of the same side is stretched downward and the tail feathers of that side are fanned out. We don't know for sure whether this is comparable to the stretching we do in the morning after waking up, but when you watch the birds you can't help thinking it is.

Yawning: Parrots yawn frequently. We think their yawning serves as a stretching exercise for the beak; as an expression of feeling tired, similar to human yawning; and/or as a mechanism to increase the intake of oxygen.

Just recently the theory has been advanced that parrots have a "yawning reflex" that causes them to yawn whenever they scratch in a certain spot (between the base of the upper beak and the ear opening). Supposedly this reflex can be activated in tame parrots by their keepers.

Resting and Sleeping

Parrots in captivity are active primarily in the early morning and late afternoon. Singly

A yellow-fronted Amazon yawning. Not unlike people, parrots yawn because they are tired, to absorb oxygen, or to stretch the muscles of their bills.

kept birds may also perk up in the evening when the entire family is at home and in the same room with them. In the hours between, parrots usually rest, sitting on one leg with closed or half-closed eyes and lightly fluffed feathers. Sometimes they turn their heads backward and tuck their bills in the shoulder feathers. Healthy adult birds sleep standing on one leg with eyes completely closed and always bury their heads in their back feathers. Youngsters and sick birds often sleep on both legs. Sick birds sleep and rest more than healthy birds, are less active in general, and remain aloof even when their cage or aviary companions are busily going through their antics (see First Signs of Illness and Measures to Take, page 42).

Social Behavior

In nature, most parrots live together in flocks, largish bands, or at least in family groups. For a number of members of a species to live together peacefully, efficiently, and without major conflicts, certain behavior patterns are necessary. To ensure smooth coexistence within a group, parrots have developed some complex and very specific patterns of behavior, the meaning of which is clearly understood by all members of the group, especially by members of the opposite sex. Vocal expression as well as sequences of movement and postures — much of which is innate — are part of this "language." Some of this "parrot etiquette" is quite commonly observed among parrots in captivity. It is especially important for owners of several birds to interpret this behavior correctly because it will give them some clues about which parrots are getting along well together and might proceed to mate and raise a family.

Mutual Preening

Parrots that have been living together for a long time in a cage or an aviary and know each other well can often be observed scratching each other's heads either simultaneously or taking turns. This form of social interaction is usually called mutual preening and satisfies the need for physical contact with another member of the species. Many

Typical sleeping posture of parrots. Parrots usually sleep on one leg. The other is drawn up into the belly feathers. The head is tucked into the back feathers.

parrot keepers simply call it "head scratching." Heterosexual bird couples often engage in mutual preening with great abandon. Mutual preening helps establish and strengthen the mating bond. Often parrots respond to unsettling events or unfamiliar objects by first turning to their partner for mutual preening. It is as though they tried to find reassurance by checking on the security of their bond before they decide to react

in any way — whether with attack, flight, or apparent disregard.

Mutual preening has another very practical function. It allows the birds to get the parts of the plumage clean that they cannot reach with their own beaks (especially the head and throat).

Parrots of the same sex also preen each other occasionally, especially if two birds live together as a pair and have no chance to form a bond with a bird of the opposite sex. The need for sociability and physical contact is so great in parrots that, if necessary, social contact is established between totally unrelated parrots. Two such birds will preen each other and sit huddled closely together when resting. Because of this same social need, parrots that are kept singly will form a close attachment to their keepers and accept them as "partners" (see page 7).

Partner Feeding

Like mutual preening, partner feeding strengthens the bond between two birds. At the same time it serves as practice for a future task, namely, that of rearing young, when the male will be responsible for feeding his mate while she incubates the eggs. When he feeds her, he regurgitates semiliquid food from his crop, often with nodding motions of the head. Then he transfers this crop milk from his bill to hers, probably moving it with the help of the tongue. Partner feeding is not often seen outside the reproductive period (see pages 70–75 for courtship, incubation, and rearing of the young).

Warning and Attack Behavior

All animal behavior directed at other members of the species connected with defense

The Behavior of Parrots

and aggression is subsumed by biologists under the term "agonism" or "agonistic behavior."

Acts of warning and attack can be observed at all times of the year, but they are far more frequent during the mating season. The closeness of the bond between a mating couple and, later, the necessity of protecting their offspring create conflict situations that inevitably give rise to aggression. Usually this aggression is only symbolically demonstrated in threatening stances or gestures; it seldom takes the form of serious fighting that results in wounds.

Threatening stance: The threatening stance is the mildest expression of aggressive intent. It is often, but not exclusively, seen during the courtship period. To appear as intimidating as possible, parrots slightly lift their wings, fan out the tail, and make the feathers on the nape stand up; cockatoos also raise their often brightly colored crests.

Threatening stance. With one foot raised, this Amazon is trying to intimidate the gray parrot and drive it off the perch.

In this posture the colorful markings of the plumage — which may be hidden when the wings are folded close to the body and the tail feathers are closed — are prominently displayed. In addition, the birds try to appear optically larger than they are to scare off potential rivals and at the same time present themselves to their intended partners in as favorable a light as possible.

Opening the beak: One of the important rules of living together in a flock is that all the birds keep a certain distance, the so-called individual distance, from each other. Every member of the flock knows exactly just how far away to stay from the others. (In contact sitting, when a pair of birds sits huddled close together, the rule of maintaining individual distance does not apply.) If a bird disregards individual distance and infringes on another's space, the latter resorts to the open beak gesture. It turns its head toward the intruder with a growling sound, opens the beak, and makes several hacking motions at the opponent without, however, actually touching it with this sharp biting tool. This behavior is not to be interpreted as an attack; it is purely a threatening gesture. The weaker bird never beats a hasty retreat but takes its time, knowing that it is in no danger of a fight.

Foot raising and foot boxing: Like the open beak gesture, foot raising and boxing are threatening acts that are primarily defensive rather than aggressive in nature. A bird that feels harassed by another raises its foot and points it toward the intruder's abdomen but shows no intention of vacating its perch. Frequently the intruder responds in kind, also raising its foot, and a regular boxing match may ensue. After such an altercation the weaker bird usually retreats.

Pecking fights: Sometimes the two threatening gestures just described lead to a pecking fight. The beak of the attacking bird is aimed at the head, shoulders, and beak of the opponent, which responds by

Pecking fights (blue and gold macaw on left, scarlet macaw on right) rarely result in serious injuries to either party.

trying to parry the attacks and defend its position. However, an innate inhibition against biting is clearly evident here — as in the open beak, threatening gesture — because both parties consistently pass up chances to hack at vulnerable parts of the opponent's body. In the end they refrain from biting even though there is no lack of opportunity.

Serious battles: Real fighting that leads to serious injuries is a rare occurrence among parrots. I was able to observe such a fight only once. Two Amazons were housed in adjacent aviaries and one day found themselves in the same compartment. They immediately pounced on each other, tumbled to the ground, and hacked at each other with loud shrieks. Even when one of them lay on its back, defending itself with beak and claws, the other would not let up and had to be forcefully removed with the help of leather gloves and a bird net.

Popular Parrot Species

In this chapter I will introduce only parrots that are more or less commonly found in pet stores or are available from parrot breeders and that are relatively easy to keep in a cage or aviary. The descriptions under the individual species give information about the appearance, distribution, natural habitat, and characteristic traits of the birds, and they include special instructions for care and breeding. The sizes given refer to the full length of adult birds, measured from the tip of the bill to the tip of the tail.

Parrots of the Pacific Distribution: Cockatoos

Cockatoos are subdivided into five genera with a total of seventeen species and are distributed over much of Australia and Indonesia. They vary in size from 12 inches (30 cm; Philippine cockatoo) to 26 inches (65 cm; palm cockatoo). (Neither of these two birds is described here because they are very rare.)

As a rule, cockatoos take longer to get used to captivity than many South and Central American parrots, but once they have adjusted they are considerably hardier and less sensitive to the cold than the latter.

If cockatoos are confined to small cages they quickly become neurotic screechers or feather pluckers. This is particularly true of the Moluccan cockatoo, which often responds badly to captivity. Even in zoos, where the birds are kept in as ideal a setting as possible, one rarely sees a Moluccan cockatoo with perfect plumage. Very spacious aviaries, not less than 15 feet (4½ m) in length, with steel grating, connected to an enclosed

room that is slightly heated, are recommended for cockatoos and are absolutely essential if the keeper hopes to breed the birds.

Greater Sulfur-Crested Cockatoo: Cacatua *galerita* (Four Subspecies)

Description: Length: 20 inches (50 cm). Male: Overall color, white; ear coverts, depending on the race, pale to deep yellow; crest and underside of wings and tail, yellow. Eyes, dark brown to black, with a ring of bare, usually white skin around them. Bill, grayish black; feet, grayish. Female: Like the male except the eyes, which turn reddish brown in the third year. The subspecies differ from each other mostly in size and in the color of the cheeks and eye rings. The triton cockatoo *(C. g. triton)* is the only cockatoo of this species with blue eye rings and snow-white cheeks.

Distribution: Northern, eastern, and southern Australia, Tasmania, New Guinea, and King and Aru islands. Introduced to New Zealand.

Habitat: Open woods and farmland, usually near moving water; occasionally also in boggy areas of tropical rain forests.

Popular Parrot Species

Aviculture: Along with the Moluccan, the greater sulfur-crested cockatoo is one of the largest members of the genus *Cacatua*. It is endowed with a powerful bill (and a matching need for gnawing), as well as a loud, strident voice. Although hand-raised males are counted among the most playful and amusing cage birds, this species' vocal powers and predilection for gnawing detract from their desirability as household pets. In addition it is hardly fair to these large creatures to keep them in a cage. If they are housed in an aviary they are among the hardiest and most adaptable parrots, and in mild climates they can winter over in unheated quarters. Make sure the quarters are dry and draft-free. Sulfur-crested cockatoos often live to a great age in captivity; the literature on cockatoos tells of some that have lived to over 100 years.

Breeding: Reports of the successful reproduction of this species in captivity are quite numerous. When courting his mate, the male fans out his tail feathers and prances along the perch toward her, nodding his head vigorously up and down with an erect crest. At the same time he emits soft chirping tones, and eventually he puts his head across hers. For the actual mating, which follows upon these preliminaries, the male either flies on top of the female or mounts her, spreading his wings wide. Usually two eggs are laid; more rarely a clutch has one egg or three. Incubation takes 30 days. One aviculturist observed a pair in which the male sat on the eggs every day from ten to eleven o'clock in the morning and from three to four o'clock in the afternoon; the rest of the time the female sat on them. The nestling period is 85 days. Even though the youngsters start eating on their own at about 100 days, the parents go on feeding them until they are 5 months old.

Lesser Sulfur-Crested Cockatoo: Cacatua sulphurea (Six Subspecies)
Photograph on page 9 and on back cover.

Description: Length: 13½ inches (34 cm). Male: Overall color, white; round ear coverts, crest, and underside of the wings and tail, yellow; eyes, very dark brown with rings of bare white skin around them; bill, black; feet, gray. The female is identical to the male. The eyes of the youngsters are grayish during the first year, pale yellow in the second, and turn reddish brown in the third. Of the six subspecies, the slightly larger citron-crested cockatoo (*C. s. citrinocristata*) is the most striking with its yellow ear coverts and orange crest.

Distribution: Celebes, Sunda islands, and the islands in the Flores and Java Seas. Probably introduced to Singapore.

Habitat: Open woods; occasionally dense forests, montane areas, and grain fields.

Aviculture: The lesser sulfur-crested cockatoo is the most popular cockatoo. In the past it was mostly kept as a tame pet bird,

Popular Parrot Species

but now many aviculturists keep and breed this parrot in aviaries. In spite of their modest size, lesser sulfur-crested cockatoos need accommodations large enough to permit flying because the birds' flying powers are well developed. Like their larger cousins, they destroy wood at an alarming rate so that their aviaries should be constructed of a very hard material, such as steel.

Breeding: Lesser sulfur-crested cockatoos are the easiest cockatoos to breed, and they are therefore an ideal subject for beginners in aviculture. They are also quite resistant to colder temperatures and in general present no problems of maintenance. Another bonus is that their sex and age are easy to determine (see Description). This facilitates the matching of pairs. It is not uncommon, however, for a pair not to hit it off at first. In bad cases the male constantly chases the female around the aviary until she either seeks refuge in the nest box or tries to get away from him by crouching on the floor. The male may even chase her away from the food so that she gets hungry and eventually collapses from exhaustion and lack of nourishment. A sufficiently large aviary is therefore essential and usually offers some opportunities for the female to evade her pursuer. In some situations it may be a good idea to reduce the male's flying agility somewhat by carefully trimming the tips of the feathers on both wings, or you may have no choice in the end but to exchange one of the birds. When trying to breed these cockatoos, the aviculturist should always make sure that the female matches the male in flying power and agility and is not in any way handicapped (as by having clipped or partially amputated wings).

As part of the courtship display, the male struts back and forth on his perch with erect crest and sometimes with spread wings, "bowing" repeatedly to his lady. Partner feeding, which is part of the courtship ritual of many African and Central and South American parrots, is unknown among the cockatoos described in this book. Later, the two parents take turns sitting on the clutch, which is made up of two or three eggs, and are thus both able to go after food. Consequently there is no biologic need for the male to feed the female during the brooding period, and in the courtship phase, partner feeding, the ritualized form of this behavior, does not form part of the courtship display in this species. The chicks hatch after 21–25 days and are ready to leave the nest at 8–10 weeks.

Moluccan Cockatoo or Salmon-Crested Cockatoo:
Cacatua moluccensis
Photograph on inside back cover.

Description: Length: 22 inches (55 cm). Male: Overall color, white, often with a hint of pink. The round crest is made up of salmon-

97

colored inner feathers peeking out between paler pink outer feathers. The bill is black; the feet, gray; the eyes, black. Female: Identical to the male except that the eyes are dark brown.

Distribution: Molucca islands, Ceram, Sapurua, Haruku, and introduced to Amboina.

Habitat: In small groups in wooded areas near the coast, especially plains and low hills up to an altitude of 3300 feet (1000 m).

Aviculture: This bird is commonly available through the pet trade, and partially tamed youngsters are sometimes offered for sale. Because of its size and general nature, the Moluccan cockatoo does not thrive in a cage. Even the indoor aviaries described on page 16 are too small for these birds. As permanent accommodations, large outdoor aviaries at least 6 feet wide are much preferable because here the birds can make at least some use of their wings. Parrot fanciers who have only seen caged Moluccan cockatoos would be amazed to see with what agility these large birds can fly. If their large wing feathers are trimmed, Moluccan cockatoos can also be kept on a climbing tree.

Breeding: Only few Moluccan cockatoos have reproduced so far in captivity. Probably the main reason for this is the nervousness of these birds. Even pairs that have formed a bond and get along well together are hardly able to settle down long enough to go about the business of breeding and raising young. Of course other factors are involved, too. Not many parrot fanciers are in a position to supply these large birds with enough space, nor do they live far enough from neighbors who might object to the birds' ear-splitting voices. And then, of course, Moluccan cocka-

toos are very expensive. A number of Moluccan cockatoos have been hand-raised, but I am aware of only four instances in the Federal Republic of Germany in which chicks were reared by their parents.

The sexes can be told apart by the color of their eyes (see Description). Usually two eggs are laid, and they are incubated for 30–35 or 36 days. The nestlings are about 3 months old when they first leave the nest.

Umbrella-Crested Cockatoo or White Cockatoo:
Cacatua alba

Drawing on page 24.

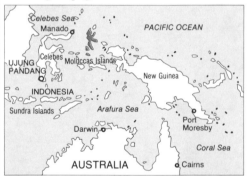

Description: Length: 18 inches (46 cm). Male: Overall color, white, including the wide-feathered crest. Eyes, dark brown to black, with creamy white, bare eye rings. Bill, black; feet, dark gray. The female resembles the male but has reddish brown eyes.

Distribution: Moluccas, Obi, Batjan, Tidore, and Ternate.

Habitat: Not known. The species lives in pairs or small groups.

Aviculture: Although umbrella-crested cockatoos are not rare either in their native habitat or in aviculture, very little is known about them. Apparently this bird is not very popular with parrot fanciers. This can be ascribed only partially, I think, to the destructiveness of its beak and its loud, penetrating voice.

Umbrella-crested cockatoos should not be kept in a cage, although I have seen some that were exceptionally tame and attached to their keepers and seemed not unhappy in spacious cages. In order to show off its beauty and elegance to the full, however, this bird should have a generous, long aviary made of very tough materials. Wood and wire mesh are bitten apart in no time. Umbrella-crested cockatoos are not daunted by cold weather, but they do need access to a lightly heated shelter.

Breeding: The first captive umbrella-crested cockatoo chicks hatched in California in 1960 in a barrel; the pair was owned by Mr. Paul Schneider (California). Further successes have been reported from England between 1968 and 1975 (at the Tropical Bird Gardens, Rhode, Somerset). I also know of three parrot fanciers in the Federal Republic of Germany whose birds produced offspring. In all cases, massive wooden nest boxes with walls about 3 inches (7–8 cm) thick were used. According to the scant literature on the subject, the courtship display is initiated by the female, who dances and hops from one leg to the other preceding the mating. An average clutch consists of two eggs, which are brooded for 29–33 days. The chicks are only about 1¼ inches (3 cm) long upon hatching and weigh slightly over half an ounce (15–18 g). By the time they are 8 weeks old they are completely covered with feathers. Adult males weigh about 24 ounces (680 g); females, about 22 ounces (620 g).

Goffin's Cockatoo: Cacatua goffini
Photograph on page 20.

Description: Length: 12¾ inches (32 cm). Male: Overall color, white; lores, pink; crest, small and round; underside of wings and tail, yellowish. Eyes, black, with grayish white, bare eye rings. Bill, whitish yellow; feet, light gray. The female looks like the male except the eyes, which are brownish red.

Distribution: This species is found exclusively on the Tanimbar islands west of New Guinea; it has been introduced to Tual in the Kai islands (Indonesia).

Aviculture: Goffin's cockatoo is one of the smallest cockatoos. Apparently this bird has not yet caught on with parrot fanciers because there has been hardly any mention of it in avicultural magazines during the past 10 years or so. This seems odd to me because Goffin's cockatoos are quite hardy, unproblematic charges if properly kept and have even been wintered over "cold," that is, in a dry, draft-free, but unheated shelter. It is true, of course, that like many of their relatives, they love chewing whatever they can get their bills on and possess powerful voices that will not endear them to neighbors.

According to my own observations and those of other cockatoo owners I know, Goffin's cockatoos are given to feather plucking if they feel too confined in their quarters; but in an outdoor aviary with an attached shelter they hardly even display this habit.

Breeding: Apparently Goffin's cockatoos reproduced for the first time in captivity in Holland in 1974 by E.G. Schulte, in a nest box that measured 10 inches (25 cm) square and 16 inches (40 cm) high. A similar success was reported in Germany in 1978 by a parrot fancier from Dortmund, West Germany. England had its first captive-bred birds in 1977.

We know very little about the reproductive behavior of Goffin's cockatoos. The courtship displays, which are apparently not nearly as spectacular as those of the greater and the lesser sulfur-crested cockatoos, are accompanied by clapping of the bill, in which both sexes engage. In the few cases in which the reproductive cycle was observed, the eggs were laid between April and June; the clutch consisted of two or three eggs, and incubation took 26 days in one case, 28 days in another. Information on the nestling period varies; some sources mention 8 weeks, others 12. Although Goffin's cockatoos have been regularly imported into Germany since about 1970 and there are presumably a fair number of these birds in the possession of parrot fanciers, information on them is practically non-existent. It seems to me time for some interest groups to be formed that would concentrate on gathering information on this unjustly neglected cockatoo and try to encourage serious breeding efforts on a larger scale. This is the only way to safeguard the survival of this species, which, because of its very limited geographic range, is especially threatened by capture for the pet trade.

Bare-Eyed Cockatoo or Little Corella: Cacatua sanguinea (Two Subspecies) Photograph on page 84.

Description: Length: 15 inches (38 cm). Male and female: Overall color, white, with a reddish tinge on the crown, forehead, nape, and throat; small, round crest; eyes of both sexes, dark brown to black, with bare, grayish blue eye rings; bill, horn-colored to white; feet, gray. The female is smaller than the male.

Eclectus parrots and long-winged parrots. ▷
Above left: Red-sided eclectus parrot. Above right: Senegal parrot. Below left: Brown parrot. Below left: Eclectus parrot (subspecies *Eclectus roratus vosmaeri*).

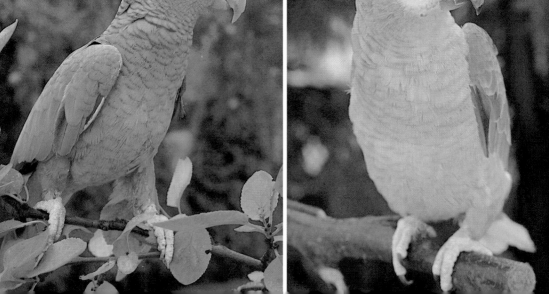

Popular Parrot Species

Distribution: The nominate subspecies, *C. s. sanguinea,* is found in eastern, north-western, and northern Australia; *C. s. normantoni,* in parts of southern New Guinea and on Cape York Peninsula and around the Gulf of Carpentaria (Australia).

Habitat: Dry inland regions and open landscapes along rivers; dense forests are largely avoided. Bare-eye cockatoos sometimes live together in huge flocks. (A flock estimated at 60,000–70,000 birds has reportedly been sighted.) Like the rose-breasted cockatoos, which are described on page 103, bare-eyed cockatoos are attracted by human settlements, penetrate into gardens and parks, and sometimes cause extensive crop damage in grain fields. For this reason they are mercilessly killed in many areas.

Aviculture: Since Australia has prohibited the export of all native fauna and flora since 1960, almost all the bare-eyed cockatoos offered for sale belong to the subspecies *C. s. normantoni* from New Guinea. Previous to 1975, bare-eyed cockatoos were only sporadically imported into Europe and America; since then they have been available in somewhat larger numbers.

Youngsters become tame very quickly, and many learn to imitate words. Bare-eyed cockatoos have a gentle and friendly disposition, but they can be raucous. Their great appetite for chewing has to be taken into consideration when choosing the building materials for an aviary.

◄ South and Central American parrots.
Above left: Bronze-winged parrot. Above right: Red-vented parrot. Below left: Spectacled Amazon. Below right: Yellow-cheeked Amazon.

Breeding: Bare-eyed cockatoos seem to breed more readily in captivity than many of their relatives. Offspring are reported relatively frequently even though these birds have not been imported in great numbers. Often cited for its successes is the San Diego Zoo in California, where one pair of bare-eyed cockatoos produced 103 young between 1929 and 1970; most of them were hand-raised. A clutch consists of two or three eggs, which are incubated for about 21 days. The nestling period is reported to be 45–50 days.

Rose-Breasted Cockatoo or Galah: Eolophus roseicapillus (Three Subspecies)
Photographs on pages 66 and 83.

Description: Length: 14 inches (35 cm). Male: Upper parts, gray; underparts, rose pink; forehead, crown, nape, and crest feathers, a delicate pink fading almost to white; under tail coverts, gray; underside of the tail, grayish black; eyes, dark brown to black; bill, yellowish gray; legs, gray. The female resembles the male but has red to reddish brown eyes.

Popular Parrot Species

Distribution: The interior of the entire Australian continent.

Habitat: Rose-breasted cockatoos are widespread in dry areas but also occur in many other types of climate and vegetation; they are often found near artificially created watering places, in parks, and in backyards.

Aviculture: Although rose-breasted cockatoos are one of the most common parrots in Australia, they are among the most sought after and expensive cockatoos in Europe. The reason for their scarcity is the strict moratorium imposed by the Australian government in the early 1960s on the export of all native fauna and flora, a moratorium that is only infrequently lifted, and then usually for purposes of scientific research. At the same time, however, Australian farmers resort to poison bait and guns in trying to control these birds because, having lost all shyness of people, they descend regularly on grain fields and are responsible for substantial crop damage. It seems highly absurd that the same birds are treated as a pest to be combated by any means on one continent while in other parts of the world they are considered precious aviary subjects.

In the meantime, rose-breasted cockatoos that have found their way to the pet market one way or another or that have been bred in aviaries command as much as $1000–$1500 a pair.

Because of the high price, the rose-breasted cockatoo is seldom found in people's homes. This is just as well, since this agile flier does much better in a spacious outdoor aviary. There it is usually quite unproblematic since it has no special demands for maintenance, is relatively hardy, and does not get sick easily. Its voice is not anywhere near as obtrusive as that of cockatoos belonging to the genus *Cacatua* so that this bird can be kept without qualms even if there are neighbors close by.

Breeding: Rose-breasted cockatoos reproduce readily, and the first domestic offspring are said to have been raised as early as the second half of the nineteenth century. During the courtship display, the male struts toward the female while bending his head forward and raising his crest. The crest, which is made up of elongated crown feathers, is not apparent when it is flattened. A brief clapping of the bill accompanies the display. Before the female gets ready to lay her eggs, the male lines the nest hole with small twigs, leaves, and bits of branches. For some strange reason he hurls every item that goes into the nest building against a hard surface before carrying it into the nest box. Ornithologists have thus far offered no convincing explanation for this behavior, though it seems conceivable that the birds are trying to get rid of any insects that might have attached themselves to the wood or leaves. A clutch consists of three to four eggs, which are brooded for 25 days alternately by both parents. The young birds are ready to leave the nest after only about 7 weeks.

Rose-breasted cockatoos have been crossed with greater sulfur-crested cockatoos, slender-billed cockatoos, Major Mitchell's cockatoo, and the Gang-gang cockatoo.

Popular Parrot Species

Eclectus Parrot:
Eclectus roratus (Ten Subspecies)
Photographs on page 101 and on back cover.

Description: Length: 14 inches (35 cm).
Male: Overall color, green; under wing coverts and sides of the body, red; edges of the wings, blue; tail, green above with blue, yellow, and white markings and gray below; eyes, orange; upper mandible, reddish orange; lower mandible, black; feet, dark gray. Female: Overall color, red; breast and abdomen, depending on the race, with bluish violet markings; tail feathers, reddish with yellow tips; wings, brownish red on top; eyes, whitish yellow; bill, black; feet, gray.

The two sexes of this species, unlike those of any other parrots described in this chapter, differ dramatically in color. The females, depending on the variety, are a spectacular combination of blue, red, and violet; the males are almost entirely green. The coloration and markings of the females are the main key to identifying the different subspecies; the males are hard to tell apart even by parrot experts. The varieties are differentiated primarily on the basis of geographic origin. Those seen most often in aviaries are the grand eclectus parrot *(E. r. roratus)* from

Ceram; the red-sided eclectus parrot *(E. r. polychloros,* previously named *E.r. pectoralis)* from New Guinea, which has blue eye rings, a blue color band, and blue on the breast and abdomen; *E. r. vosmaeri,* which resembles the nominate form; *E. r. aruensis;* and the Solomon eclectus parrot *(E. r. solomonensis).* The last two look much like the red-sided eclectus parrot.

Distribution: The Moluccan, Lesser Sunda, Tanimbar, Aru, and Kai islands; New Guinea, including surrounding islands, and Cape York in Australia.

Habitat: Low-lying plains, especially tropical rain forests. When food is abundant, eclectus parrots gather in large flocks and forage together.

Aviculture: Eclectus parrots, especially when kept singly, are placid and almost lazy birds that quickly become tame and, according to my own experience, hardly ever bite even if they are grabbed with two hands. They need an aviary with plenty of tree limbs and branches because they would rather climb than fly. The materials used in the construction of their quarters need not be exceptionally tough because eclectus parrots are not great gnawers.

Eclectus parrots should be fed primarily on fruit, corn, cooked rice, sprouts and greens. The kind of birdseed mixture that generally makes up most parrots' basic diet should be given to eclectus parrots only as a supplement — never as the only food for any length of time. Because of the variety of foods, the droppings of eclectus parrots are of course somewhat runnier than those of seed-eating birds.

Breeding: If you hope for offspring from your birds, you should watch the female with

Popular Parrot Species

special attention because she may stir up trouble in the aviary and fight for weeks before settling down with her partner. That is why it is important that the male bird you hope she will accept should be her equal in strength. If the birds are kept in an outdoor aviary, the female will start laying her eggs in April or May; indoors the mating cycle may start at any time of year except while the birds molt. Two broods per year are by no means unheard of. There are usually only two eggs in a clutch, and the female sits on them for 28 days without relief from the male. By the time the young birds are 8 weeks old, they have a full set of feathers, and by 12–13 weeks they start finding their own food.

Eclectus parrots have been successfully and quite often bred for some years so that domestically raised youngsters should become available for sale with increasing frequency in the future.

The Parrots of Africa: Long-Winged Parrots

The parrot genus *Poicephalus,* sometimes, especially in Germany, referred to as long-winged parrots, includes eight species. All these parrots are from Africa and measure about 9 inches (23 cm), except the Cape or brown-necked parrot *(P. robustus),* which is in danger of becoming extinct and measures about 13 inches (33 cm).

With the exception of the yellow-faced parrot *(P. flavifrons),* all members of the genus *Poicephalus* have been imported into Europe and America, but only the Senegal parrot is commonly available. Of the other species, only the brown parrot and Jardine's parrot appear occasionally in pet stores.

Once they are acclimated, long-winged parrots turn out to be quite hardy and can be wintered over in temperatures as low as 41°F (5°C) without suffering ill effects.

All the parrots of this group are swift and agile fliers that need plenty of space. When constructing an aviary for them, you should not be fooled by their modest size and use lighter materials than those generally recommended for parrot housing. These relatively small birds have beaks that can make short shrift of wood and thin, cheap wire. An aviculturist told me that a Senegal parrot of his managed in no time at all to make its way out of an outdoor aviary enclosed with chicken wire.

The diet of long-winged parrots is like that of other parrots (see page 35) but should contain a somewhat larger proportion of small seeds. These birds are especially fond of fruits and vegetables, which should be a steady part of their diet.

Senegal Parrot: Poicephalus senegalus (Three Subspecies)
Photograph on page 101.

Description: Length: 9 inches (23 cm). Male and female: Forehead and crown, dark gray, which turns somewhat lighter on the cheeks. Upper parts and breast, rich green; wings, olive green; underparts, yellow to orange (tending more to red in the scarlet-bellied Senegal parrot, *P. s. versteri*). Tail, olive brown; bill, grayish black; eyes, yellow; legs, brownish gray.

Popular Parrot Species

Measuring only about 9 inches, the Senegal parrot is clearly much below the average size of the so-called large parrots, but it is included in this group because of its appearance and behavioral traits.

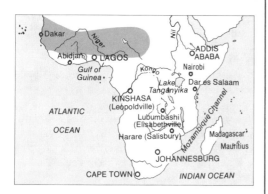

Distribution: Chad, Nigeria, Dahomey, Togo, Ghana, Upper Volta, Ivory Coast, Mali, Guinea, and Senegal.

Habitat: Dry, sparsely wooded savannas and open forests.

Aviculture: Most of the Senegal parrots sold belong to the nominate form *(P. s. senegalus)*. These birds are quite common in aviaries, and most pet stores have them for sale at most times of year. They have been selling for less than $100 for several years, so that this parrot is affordable even for fanciers with a modest pocketbook. If you are in the market for a Senegal parrot, make sure you pick a young bird (with dark eyes); stay away from adult birds, which are often offered for sale and which are easily recognizable by their yellow to orange eyes. Older birds are not recommended either as pet birds or as breeding stock. Senegal parrots that were mature when captured are obsti-

nate and ornery and will remain so. It is foolish to hope that they will at some point change their ways, become hand-tame, and accept treats from their keeper's hand.

Youngsters, on the other hand, quickly overcome their shyness and will become tame enough to live in a cage; some may even become hand-tame if the owner spends a lot of time with them. I would like to emphasize, however, that in all the years I have been studying parrots I have encountered only one Senegal parrot that was truly tame and had a close relationship with its owner.

Breeding: For many years aviculturists agreed that Senegal parrots would not — or would practically never — produce offspring in captivity, but in recent times there have been a few successful attempts in Europe. The difficulties can be attributed in part at least to the fact that most of the birds chosen for reproduction were originally caught in the wild. They find it hard to adjust to life in a cage or aviary and are so nervous that they hardly ever settle down and relax enough to come into breeding condition.

I would advise even more strongly than I do for other kinds of parrots that if you want to breed long-winged parrots you should acquire several young birds and house them together in a large aviary, thus offering them at least some choice of partners.

A clutch consists of up to four eggs, which are brooded 22–25 days. The young birds leave the nest after an average of 60 days. At that point they differ from their parents only in size, in the somewhat more muted tone of their plumage, and in the darker shade of their eyes.

Popular Parrot Species

Brown Parrot or Meyer's Parrot:
Poicephalus meyeri (Six Subspecies)
Photograph on page 101.

Description: Length: 8½ inches (22 cm). Male and female: Head, neck, upper parts, wings, and tail, grayish brown. Back and underparts, bluish green; crown, shoulder patches, thighs, and underwing coverts, yellow; bill, grayish black; legs, blackish; eyes, red. In youngsters the yellow markings are less pronounced.

Distribution: Central and eastern Africa, from Chad and the Sudan in the north to Zambia and Zimbabwe in the south. A small colony of the subspecies *P. m. transvaalensis* has established itself in southern South Africa near Port Elisabeth. Presumably the ancestors were escaped cage birds.

Habitat: Sparsely wooded savannas, trees along rivers, and even some cultivated areas.

Aviculture: Although not as common as the Senegal parrot, the brown parrot, or Meyer's parrot, is fairly well-known among parrot fanciers. Young birds lose their shyness quickly and learn to trust their caretakers, whereas birds that were mature at capture remain shy or aloof for the rest of their lives. Brown parrots require the same kind of care as Senegal parrots. According to owners, brown parrots enjoy baths.

Breeding: Brown parrots have repeatedly been bred in captivity. The most recent report (1985) is from the Federal Republic of Germany. In the hatchery of M. Gründig, three chicks hatched in 1980 after an incubation period of about 21 days. The nestling period was about 60 days. (The average incubation period is probably 27 days.) Unlike most other aviculturists who were unable to detect any clear-cut differences between the sexes of their birds, Gründig reports that his female had a wider yellow headband than the male. By the time young brown parrots leave the nest they look much like their parents except for the yellow on the head.

Jardine's Parrot:
Poicephalus gulielmi (Four Subspecies)

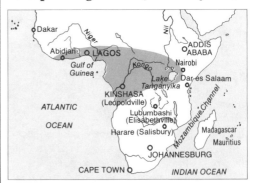

Description: Length: 11 inches (28 cm). Male and female: Overall color, green; forehead, bend of wing, and thighs, orange-red; head and back feathers, black with dark green margins; lores, large wing feathers, and tail, black; eyes, dark gray, with bare,

108

pale pink eye rings; upper mandible, horn-colored, darker toward the tip; lower mandible, black; feet, grayish brown. Youngsters lack the orange-red markings, and their eye rings are dark gray.

Distribution: Central Africa, from the Sudan and Uganda in the east to the Atlantic coast in the west; also parts of Nigeria, Dahomey, Togo, Ghana, and the Ivory Coast.

Habitat: Primarily mountain forests up to about 12,000 feet (3500 m); occasionally found in tropical forests in the plains and on coffee plantations.

Aviculture: Before 1975, hardly any private fanciers owned Jardine's parrots, and these parrots could be admired only in a few zoos and bird parks. Then they suddenly became more available for awhile, but since 1982 imports have dried up, so that now one finds these birds advertised only infrequently in avicultural magazines.

Youngsters adjust to their human keepers quickly, but birds that grew up in the wild usually stay shy for the rest of their lives and can be tamed only minimally. More than other large parrots, Jardine's parrots seem to have a tendency for feather plucking in captivity. I can attest to this myself: I had a pair of these parrots that regularly started to pluck their feathers at a certain time of year, almost invariably from February to April. Then they would stop and grow a perfect set of feathers in the following weeks and months. However, in February of the next year they would go at it again. Presumably this "bad habit" can be attributed to some dietary deficiency because, in spite of great efforts on my part, the birds ate almost exclusively dry seeds. In 1983, a parrot fancier reported similar experiences in a magazine for aviculturists. She

tried everything to stop the feather plucking but only when she finally succeeded in getting her birds used to a varied diet did the feather plucking abate.

Breeding: I am at this point aware of five breeders from four different countries (the Federal Republic of Germany, the German Democratic Republic, Switzerland, and England) who have successfully bred Jardine's parrots. The clutch of the "English" parrots contained four eggs; that of the "Swiss" birds, three. The incubation period is 26 days, and the nestling period ranges from eight to ten weeks.

African Gray Parrot:
Psittacus erithacus (Two Subspecies)
Photographs on pages 10, 20, and 66, and on back cover.

Description: Length: 14 inches (36 cm). Male and female: Overall color, gray; feathers on crown, forehead, nape, neck, and throat have lighter colored margins. Bare skin around the eyes, whitish; tail, red; bill, black; feet, gray. The eyes of immature birds are gray but change to a light grayish yellow after a few months and eventually to pale yellow.

The Timneh parrot (*P. e. timneh*), which like the nominate form (*P. e. erithacus*) is commonly imported, has a horn-colored upper mandible and brown to russet tail feathers. It measures only about 12½ inches (32 cm) and is thus clearly smaller than the nominate variety. The so-called Congo, Ghana, Cameroon, and Togo gray parrots sold by pet dealers are invariably members of the nominate subspecies.

Distribution: Equatorial Africa from the Ivory Coast in the west to western Kenya in the east, and south as far as northern Angola, southern Congo, and northwestern Tanzania.

Habitat: Forested plains. Birds go on foraging excursions to sparsely wooded savannas and to open country. Occasionally, they are also found in mangrove swamps near the coast. The gray parrot's distribution is largely identical to the range of the African oil palm, the fruit of which forms the bulk of the bird's diet.

Aviculture: The gray parrot is one of the most fascinating large parrots, not because of its plumage, which is relatively sober in color, but because of its well-known talent for mimicry. It is surpassed in this respect only by the mynah and some Corvidae. Talented gray parrots can learn not only words and phrases but also imitate sounds they hear often, such as the telephone ringing or a door creaking. The ability of gray parrots to use words appropriate to a situation, that is, the ability to respond to an event with words that make sense in that context — like "good morning" at the first meeting of the day, "good night" at the last eye contact in the evening, and "hello" when the telephone rings — has led many owners to believe that their birds understand what they say. This is not the case, however. Parrots simply imitate sounds; they echo what they hear the way all mimicking birds do. Because of their high intelligence, however, gray parrots are able to associate certain words or phrases with regularly recurring events and thus startle the observer with words appropriate to the situation. I have to stress, however, that only few gray parrots have such a highly developed talent. An extremely tame and friendly Timneh gray parrot that belongs to relatives of mine and that I look after in the summer has been saying his name, Jako, and four other similar sounding words. These few words he learned quite readily some years ago but has since obstinately refused to add to this rudimentary vocabulary in spite of many intensive training sessions. He does, however, have a fairly impressive repertoire of all the sounds that can regularly be heard near his cage.

It should also be said that not all gray parrots grow tame. Chances are best for immature birds whose eyes are still dark. Birds that were mature when caught always remain stubborn and distrustful and never become friendly with their keepers, often greeting them with growls or raucous screams.

If these sensitive parrots are kept in cages, they quickly take up the habit of feather plucking. Next to large macaws and cockatoos, African gray parrots are the greatest feather pluckers. All these birds are among the most intelligent parrots. It is no wonder that they find it hard to put up with being locked in a cage, to accept different food from that they are used to, and to tolerate the boredom that characterizes life in most cages and aviaries. Plucking their own feathers and sometimes even biting their own skin is simply a way to "blow off steam," a way to vent the aggressions, unsatisfied needs, and frustrations that build up under these conditions. If gray parrots are confined to the indoors, especially in narrow cages, a special effort should be made to offer them things that will amuse them, such as chains, branches, ends of rope, stones, and small pieces of wood they can play with and nibble on. A better idea is to keep them in an outdoor aviary with access to a lightly heated shelter.

Breeding: Both varieties of gray parrots reproduce quite commonly in captivity. If their basic needs are met (see page 109), these birds readily proceed to breed in outdoor aviaries as well as in cages. A clutch consists of three or four — rarely five — eggs, which the female broods by herself for about 30 days. The nestling period is 11–12 weeks.

Gray parrots are quite often hand-raised, especially since broody birds sometimes make some false starts before they follow through and rear their young themselves.

Parrots of the South American Distribution: Amazons

There are twenty-seven different species of Amazons distributed over the tropical regions of Central and South America and the islands of the West Indies. Because of the destruction of their natural habitat, many species are now seriously endangered, and eleven species are listed in Appendix I of the most recent edition of the Washington Convention.

The Amazons' pleasant disposition, beautiful colors, ability to adapt to life in a cage or aviary, and talent for imitating have always earned them a special place in the hearts of parrot fanciers, who in the past kept these birds primarily as indoor pets. In recent times many aviculturists have concentrated more on trying to breed Amazons, and now we are beginning to hear and read with increasing frequency of offspring born in captivity.

After acclimation, which requires considerable good judgment on the part of the importer, Amazons, with practically no exception, become unproblematic pets that can, because of their minimal flying needs, be housed either in spacious indoor quarters or in outdoor aviaries. If the birds are kept outdoors, it is important that they always have access to a dry, draft-free shelter that is lightly heated during the winter. An Amazon aviary should be constructed of tough materials that withstand the birds' strong beaks and should contain many-forked climbing trees and plenty of branches of varying thickness, so that the inhabitants can reach any point in the aviary "on foot." Especially the blue-fronted, yellow-fronted, and mealy Amazons are unenthusiastic about flying and would rather climb than make use of their wings.

There are twenty-seven Amazon species, but only three are at present imported regularly and another five at unpredictable intervals, all of them in small numbers. The more stringent import and export restrictions have had an especially drastic effect on the availability of parrots from South and Central America.

Popular Parrot Species

Spectacled Amazon or White-Fronted Amazon:
Amazona albifrons (Three Subspecies)
Photograph on page 102.

Description: Length: 10½ inches (27 cm). Male: Plumage mostly green. Forehead, white; crown, greenish blue; area around the eyes and lores, red; eyes, yellowish, with bare, grayish white eye rings; shoulder patches, red; bill, yellowish; legs, light gray. The female looks like the male but lacks the red alula and primary coverts, which are green. The spectacled Amazon is the only Amazon, together with the rare yellow-lored Amazon (*A. xantholora*), which is not described in this book — in which the color pattern of the plumage differs between males and females.

Distribution: From the western coast of Mexico across Guatemala, Honduras, and El Salvador to western Costa Rica.

Habitat: Primarily dry woods made up of bushes and deciduous trees; only rarely found in tropical rain forests. In pairs or small groups, but "also with thousands together in certain roosting spots" (Vriends).

Aviculture: Because of the decline of these birds in the wild, especially in Mexican populations, the spectacled Amazon is now, unlike in former times, offered for sale only rarely. In addition, among the birds received by importers, males usually far outnumber the females so that it is difficult to find a pair. According to many observations, captive spectacled Amazons remain quite withdrawn or shy, especially if they were mature when caught. Immature birds, which can be spotted by the yellowish color of their crown, take relatively well to their keepers and to life in a cage or aviary. They are said to have some talent for mimicking.

Breeding: To my knowledge, the first domestic chicks were born in 1949 in the United States by I.D. Putman; the second in 1977 in the Federal Republic of Germany by H. Müller (Walsrode), and a third set in Switzerland in 1979; since then several European aviculturists have reported breeding successes. The last report came in in 1985 from the bird park Metelen Heide in Muensterland (West Germany). There a clutch of five eggs produced four hatchlings in mid-June 1984 after an incubation period of 28 days. The fully fledged young left the nest after about 70 days but were still actively looked after and fed, mostly by the male parent, for a few more weeks.

Popular Parrot Species

Green-Cheeked Amazon or Mexican Red-Headed Amazon:
Amazona viridigenalis

Description: Length: 13½ inches (33 cm). Male and female: Plumage, mostly green; crown and forehead, red; a crescent-shaped, bluish violet band behind cheeks; red and blue primaries; bill, yellowish, with white ceres; legs, gray; eyes, yellow, with bare, white eye rings.

Distribution: Only northeastern Mexico.

Habitat: Wooded areas along rivers, grain fields in low-lying, wet plains, dry hill crests with scattered pines, and tropical forests in canyons.

Aviculture: Green-cheeked Amazons are no longer imported at all or only as an exception. Specialists assume that this bird will shortly be added to the list of endangered species (Appendix I of the Washington Convention). In the United States, however, this gentle bird is still extremely popular.

This particular Amazon behaves quite differently from other species of the genus. Green-cheeked Amazons in captivity are very calm, almost lethargic, and move as though in slow motion. Only in the early morning and in the evening do they come to life and make free use of their loud and penetrating voices.

Breeding: Green-cheeked Amazons have been bred in captivity a number of times in recent years. The first successes were scored in the 1970s in Africa and in England; in the United States young were reared at the Los Angeles Zoo in 1970. In Texas, P. Springman reared many young from two pairs, since 1972; in 1976, second-generation young were reared! In 1981, pairs of green-cheeked Amazons reproduced in Sweden and Switzerland. The first "German" green-cheeked Amazons were raised in 1982 at the Private Institute for Parrot Research in Oberhausen. For several years the parent birds, which had not been definitely sexed (by endoscopy; see page 58), had shown no interest in mating when, in the spring of 1981, they enacted their courtship display, laid eggs, and brooded them. The single nestling that hatched was killed by the parent birds one night during a thunderstorm. The following year the female laid two eggs in early May, and the two chicks that hatched after 28 days were raised by both parents. When the fledglings left the nest box after about 70 days, they had a full set of feathers and looked much like their parents. The only differences were that they were clearly smaller, that they had only a narrow band of red across the forehead, and that they lacked the characteristic blue crescent on the cheeks. The eyes of the youngsters were a muddy, grayish yellow. At about 120 days the young birds began to feed themselves.

Popular Parrot Species

Finsch's Amazon:
Amazona finschi (Two Subspecies)

Description: Length: 13½ inches (33 cm). Male and female: Overall color, green with darker margins on the feathers of the neck and underparts; forehead and lores, reddish brown; crown, nape, and some feathers forming a crescent on the cheek, bluish white; wings, bluish black; eyes, orange; bill, horn-colored; feet, gray.

Distribution: Western Mexico.

Habitat: Plains, wooded mountain regions up to about 7000 feet (2200 m) above sea level, and occasionally cultivated fields and banana plantations.

Aviculture: From 1975 to 1982 Finsch's parrots were routinely imported to Europe and America, but in recent years they have been found only rarely through the pet trade or through advertisements in avicultural magazines. Finsch's parrots lose their shyness of people less quickly than many related species, and my own experience has been that even immature birds don't develop much trust. The experience of having been caught apparently affects them permanently and causes them to be nervous and fright-ened in situations that would leave blue-fronted, yellow-cheeked, or yellow-fronted Amazons quite unruffled. In my opinion, however, Finsch's parrots display one of the loveliest color combinations, and I would not want to miss them in my aviaries even though they don't adjust as easily to life in captivity as do some other Amazons. However, I think that they are not suitable for a cage despite that some birds that were acquired very young may develop into pleas-ant pet parrots.

Breeding: Very little is known about the breeding behavior of Finsch's parrots. All the literature on offspring raised in captivity (often hand-raised) has appeared in English-language publications. Incubation is reported to last 28 days, and the youngsters leave the nest at about 8 weeks.

Yellow-Cheeked Amazon:
Amazona autumnalis (Four Subspecies)
See photograph on page 102.

Description: Length: 13½ inches (34 cm). Male and female: Overall color, bright green; forehead and lores, scarlet; crown and a few neck feathers, light blue; cheeks, yellow; wing speculum, red; primaries, bluish black; bill, dark horn color; feet, gray; eyes golden to dark brown, surrounded by bare, white eye rings. Salvin's Amazon (*A. a. salvini*) lacks the yellow cheeks; Lesson's Amazon (*A. a. lilacina*) has a bluish lilac crown; green ear coverts, and yellowish green neck and cheek areas. The diademed Amazon (*A. a. diadema*) resembles Salvin's amazon but has small, red, hairlike feathers on the ceres.

Distribution: The nominate form (*A. a. autumnalis*) is found along the east coast of Mexico, on the Belize peninsula, in Guatemala, and in Honduras; Salvin's Amazon, in Nicaragua, Costa Rica, Panama, and on the west coast of Colombia; Lesson's Amazon, exclusively in Ecuador. The diademed Amazon lives in the interior of Brazil, more than 600 miles farther east.

Habitat: Low-lying tropical forests and areas bordering forests.

Aviculture: Of the four subspecies only the nominate form is occasionally available for purchase. Salvin's and Lesson's Amazons are at this point imported only rarely, and the diademed Amazon practically not at all, although it might occasionally be mistaken for a Salvin's Amazon (see Description) and enter the country that way. Diademed Amazons that are sometimes advertised in avicultural magazines are almost never newly imported but are offered for sale by private owners.

All subspecies of *A. autumnalis* take to life in a cage or aviary without difficulty and quickly become tame. But birds of this species have some of the most powerful voices of all amazons, and their piercing, monotonous, and persistent song, which is repeated several times in the course of a day, can wear down even nerves of steel.

Breeding: So far *A. autumnalis* has reproduced in captivity only rarely. One of the first documented cases dates back to 1946, when a pair of Lesson's Amazons are said to have produced offspring in the United States. In 1956, the Englishman E. N. T. Vane had a similar and often cited success with yellow-cheeked Amazons. He placed the fertilized eggs of a pair of yellow-cheeked Amazons, which had been laying eggs for several years but never produced chicks, in the nest of a single African gray parrot hen that was sitting on a clutch of her own (obviously infertile) eggs. After 26 days one chick hatched and was raised by its unrelated foster mother.

To my knowledge the first yellow-cheeked Amazon chicks (of the nominate subspecies *A. a. autumnalis*) to be raised by their parents belonged to S. Maindok of Alzey in the Federal Republic of Germany. His birds produced young in 1983. Another subspecies, the rare Salvin's Amazon *(A. a. Salvini),* has been successfully raised by the German breeder K. H. Uhlenkott of Ahaus and by the Rostock Zoo in the Democratic Republic of Germany.

Blue-Fronted Amazon:
Amazona aestiva (Two Subspecies)
Photographs on page 65 and on back cover.

Description: Length: 15 inches (37 cm). Male and female: Overall color, green; forehead and lores, light blue; crown and eye region and in some individuals the throat, breast, and thighs, yellow; bend of wing, red, usually interspersed with yellow; wing speculum and base of the tail feathers, red; eyes, red to orange, with bare, grayish blue eye rings; bill, black; feet, bluish gray.

Popular Parrot Species

In the subspecies *A. a. xanthopteryx*, known as the yellow-winged Amazon, the bend of wing is predominantly yellow.

Distribution: The blue-fronted Amazon is found in large parts of Brazil, whereas the yellow-winged lives in northern Bolivia, parts of Brazil, Paraguay, and northern Argentina.

Habitat: Primarily forests. Blue-fronted Amazons live in large flocks and are sometimes found together with orange-winged Amazons. All the birds of the flock spend the night together in a communal sleeping place and then set off in the early morning for their favorite feeding grounds.

Aviculture: Apart from the African gray parrot, the blue-fronted Amazon is probably the most popular large parrot. The various subspecies of the yellow-fronted Amazon are the only other parrots that are close in terms of numbers imported. Blue-fronted Amazons are reputed to be excellent mimics of human speech and other sounds, although their speaking talent by no means matches that of African grays.

It is only in recent years that blue-fronted Amazons have been kept extensively in avi-aries. Before now, these birds were imported by the thousands to become pets in European and American homes. They proved to be adaptable, adjusting to their new existence quickly and often becoming tame and friendly indoor birds.

An aviary designed for blue-fronted Amazons should be built of good, strong metal even though many Amazons of this species hardly ever or never gnaw on objects, and aviaries with wooden framing may hold up for a long time without being damaged by the parrots' beaks. Judging from my experience, blue-fronted Amazons are some of the hardiest of their genus, but they still should not spend the winter in completely unheated quarters. If it gets too cold, their feet can freeze, which in bad cases can lead to the partial loss of toes.

Breeding: Only in recent years, since imports have been restricted and parrot populations have been decimated in their native habitat, have aviculturists tried seriously to breed blue-fronted Amazons. This species does not reproduce at all easily in captivity, as the paucity of breeding reports and the small number of birds advertised attest. R. Low, an English parrot expert and author of parrot books, estimates that there are only about a dozen breeding pairs in England. The situation is just as bad, if not worse, in the United States, although some young have been reared at Poer Bird Farm, Phoenix. For sexing birds, we have to rely primarily on behavioral clues. Intensive mutual preening, partner feeding, and attempts to mate may be signs of a sexual bond between two birds. The male usually initiates the courtship display. He woos his mate with narrowed pupils, fanned tail, raised neck feathers, and erect stance. She in turn indicates her readiness to mate by crouching low on her perch, vibrating her wings, and emitting chirping sounds. A clutch usually contains between two and five eggs, which are incubated — like those of many other Amazon species — for 28–30 days. The nestlings leave the nest after 55–60 days.

Yellow-Fronted Amazon or Yellow-Crowned Amazon:
Amazona ochrocephala (Nine Subspecies) Photograph on inside front cover and back cover.

Description: Length: 14 inches (35 cm). Male and female: Overall color, green; crown (and sometimes the forehead), yellow; bend of wing and speculum, light red; underside of tail, yellowish green with a red dot at the base of each tail feather; eyes, orange, with bare, white eye rings; bill, dark gray, with the upper mandible pink toward the base; feet, gray.
Distribution: South America, from Guiana and Venezuela in the east to the Colombian Andes in the west; also Trinidad.

The Panama Amazon (*A. o. panamensis*) resembles the nominate form but has a yellow forehead, a horn-colored bill with a dark-tipped upper mandible, and flesh-colored feet. The entire bird is somewhat smaller (13 inches; 33 cm).
Distribution: Panama and the tropical lowlands of northern Colombia.

The yellow-naped Amazon (*A. o. auropalliata*) also resembles the nominate form but has a yellow nape, a grayish to horn-colored bill, gray eye rings, and flesh-colored feet and is larger (15½ inches or 39 cm).
Distribution: Central America, from southwestern Mexico to Costa Rica.

The Mexican double yellow head (*A. o. oratrix*) differs from the yellow-fronted by having a completely yellow head and neck; the bill is entirely horn-colored, the feet are lighter, and the bird is larger (16½ inches or 41 cm).
Distribution: Mexico.

A. o. belizensis resembles the Mexican double head but has less yellow on the head.
Distribution: Honduras.

The other varieties are imported only rarely or are incorrectly identified at import and are therefore not described here.

Aviculture: Even a few years ago a number of varieties of *A. ochrocephala* were carried quite regularly by pet dealers, but this has changed as a consequence of sharp tightening of import and export regulations, so that now these Amazons come up for sale only rarely when someone decides to sell a bird that is already in the country.

This Amazon species includes birds with an excellent disposition and often a gift for talking. Some of them are as good as an African gray parrot of average talent, but the imitations produced by Amazons are always more distorted than those of an African gray.

Yellow-fronted Amazons can be kept in either a cage or an outdoor aviary, although to me the latter kind of housing seems preferable. When they live in an aviary they fly about actively. Their voices are among the loudest within the Amazon group, and their need to chew, causing destruction to aviary and other objects, is enormous. Apart from these "faults," the varieties just described are all highly recommended for fanciers. Immature birds, in particular, develop into the most affectionate, playful, and amusing pets imaginable.

Breeding: Several subspecies of this Amazon have been known to reproduce in captivity, although none of them in substantial numbers. There are three or four eggs in a clutch, and the incubation period is about 26–28 days. The fully fledged young birds leave the nest box 12 weeks after hatching.

Orange-Winged Amazon:
Amazona amazonica (Three Subspecies)
Description: Length: 13 inches (32 cm). Male and female: Overall color, green; crown and forehead have irregular blue and yellow markings; cheeks, yellow; wing margins, yellowish green; wing speculum, red; tail feathers, green with some red on the proximal vanes of the outer feathers; bill, horn-colored, darkening toward the tip; feet, gray; eyes, yellow to orange, surrounded by bare, gray eye rings.

Distribution: All of northern South America with the exception of the Andes region in the west and coastal areas in east-ern Brazil; farther south, parts of Bolivia and the northern tip of Paraguay.

Habitat: Wet forests and mangrove swamps.

Aviculture: The distribution of blue and yellow on the head differs markedly from bird to bird, as it does in the blue-fronted Amazon (see page 115). The two species are therefore often confused even though there is a clear difference in size. Next to the different varieties of yellow-fronted and blue-fronted Amazons, the orange-winged is the most common Amazon found in cages and aviaries. At present (1986), probably more than half of all imported Amazons are orange-winged. This species takes readily to life in a cage or aviary and quickly overcomes its natural shyness.

Breeding: Although this Amazon is popular with fanciers and aviculturists, it has reproduced only very rarely. There are no

Large macaws.
Above left: Scarlet macaw. Above right: Pair of blue and gold macaws. Below left: Military macaws. Below right: A bonded pair of green-winged macaws.

clear, reliable differences between the sexes, although one aviculturist claims that the blue markings on the head are more pronounced in the male and that the females have larger yellow cheek patches than the males.

The first aviculturist in German-speaking Europe to report breeding orange-winged Amazons is A. Mitterhuber of Weil, Baden Wuerttemberg. In 1978, his birds produced three eggs in the first days of June. Two chicks hatched in early July. Their eyes opened at about 3 weeks, and in the sixth week the flight feathers began to grow in. At 8 weeks the first small yellow feathers appeared on the head, and 2 weeks later the plumage was almost complete. Another aviculturist, C. Ott, whose orange-headed Amazons produced young in 1982, reports that the fledglings first emerged from their nest box at about 8 weeks and were already starting to find their own food at 11 weeks.

Mealy Amazon:

Amazona farinosa (Five Subspecies)

Description: Length: 15½–16 inches (38–40 cm). Male and female: Overall color, green; upper parts green with a grayish, powdery, or "mealy" look; some feathers on the crown are yellow; wing margins and

◄ Small macaws and caiques.
Above left. Severe macaw. Above right: Yellow-naped macaw. Below left: Black-headed caique. Below right: White-bellied caique.

speculum, red; yellowish green band at the end of the tail; eyes, brownish red, with bare, white eye rings; bill, dark horn color with a yellowish area at the base of the upper mandible; feet, gray.

The subspecies *A. f. inornata* (plain-colored Amazon) lacks the yellow on the crown, and *A. f. guatemalae* (blue-crowned Amazon) has a bluish crown and neck.

Distribution: From Mexico to the Atlantic coast in southern Brazil; also northwestern South America.

Habitat: Open rain forests and along the edge of forests; dense, junglelike forests are largely avoided.

Aviculture: For a number of years mealy Amazons came on the market only sporadically, but since 1983 this bird has been imported more frequently. (It now ranks third among all the Amazons in terms of numbers imported, coming after the blue-fronted and the orange-winged Amazons.)

In vocal power the mealy Amazon is second only to the yellow-fronted. An ornithologist who had the opportunity of observing these birds in the wild claims their calls can be heard from more than a kilometer away.

Popular Parrot Species

Except for this rather undesirable trait, mealy Amazons make excellent cage or aviary birds. They become tame quickly and are said to be talented mimics. My own experience is limited to two specimens of the nominate variety. Both birds were hand-tamed and were initially housed together with two young Mexican double yellow heads. The latter soon asserted dominance in the aviary and "oppressed" the mealies even though both sets of birds were equal in size. The Mexican double yellow heads drove the mealies away from the food and chased them constantly, and I quickly realized that the mealies had to be moved to an aviary of their own.

Breeding: There are hardly any success stories about breeding mealy Amazons, probably because these birds have been so irregularly imported in the past. To my knowledge, the first aviculturist to have successfully bred this species is W. Burkart of Benningen, Federal Republic of Germany, whose birds (*A. f. guatemalae*) produced offspring in 1984.

Parrots of the *Pionus* Genus

Of the eight species belonging to the *Pionus* genus, only the red-vented, Maximilian's, and the bronze-winged parrots are sometimes available for sale. Other species appear unpredictably, usually arriving in Europe as part of an import shipment of other parrots. All *Pionus* parrots have red feathers on the underside of the tail near the vent. In a number of species the small feathers on the head, breast, and abdomen are white at the base so that when the plumage is not in top condition, as during molt, the white shows through, detracting from the bird's looks. G. A. Smith, a well-known English veterinarian and parrot specialist, has put forth the hypothesis that the white on the feather base, which is left when the dark tips break off during excessively vigorous mutual preening, has the function of inhibiting aggression. According to him, these white feather bases signal to a bird that is grooming the head of another when to stop or proceed more gently.

Pionus parrots bear up under the strains of transport and officially prescribed quarantine much less well than their relatives, the Amazons. Freshly imported parrots of this group are quite susceptible to all kinds of diseases. Many succumb during the first few weeks to aspergillosis, a fungus infection (see page 45). Since this condition becomes apparent only at an advanced stage, it is usually too late for successful treatment. Once the fungus has spread to the upper respiratory tract, the birds suffer increasingly from shortness of breath, which manifests itself in labored breathing accompanied by audible wheezing and a noticeable rising and falling of the diaphragm and tail with every breath.

It should be mentioned, however, that many *Pionus* parrots also start breathing heavily — as though they were seriously sick — when they are excited, during mating time, and at critical moments as when dogs, cats, or unfamiliar people get too close for comfort. The external symptoms produced at such times are practically indistinguishable from those of aspergillosis.

Once *Pionus* parrots have been carefully acclimated, they are pleasant cage or aviary birds. If confined to too small a cage they

Popular Parrot Species

can be quite lethargic. An aviary about 6 feet (2 m) long with an attached shelter is suitable for all members of this genus. Generally these birds get along quite well with other members of their species and genus as well as with different parrots and even quite unrelated birds, if there is enough room in the aviary to get out of each other's way. A large enough outdoor aviary can be planted; these birds will not harm the plants much by chewing on them. The temperature should not drop below 50–54°F (10–12°C). *Pionus* parrots have quite inoffensive voices, but their talent for talking is negligible.

Red-Vented Parrot or Blue-Headed Parrot:
Pionus menstruus (Three Subspecies)
Photograph on page 102.

Description: Length: 11 inches (28 cm). Male and female: Overall color, green; head, neck, and throat, dark blue, with mauve margins on some of the throat feathers; ear coverts, black; wing coverts, olive green; undertail coverts, red with green tips; tail, red at the base, otherwise green; distal vanes of outer tail feathers, blue; eyes, dark brown, surrounded by bare, gray eye rings; bill, black with a small pink area at the base of the upper mandible; feet, gray.

Distribution: From Costa Rica to northern Bolivia and Brazil; also Trinidad.

Habitat: Tropical, low-lying forests. Even the extensive habitat destruction and the pet trade have thus far not significantly affected the huge populations. Red-vented parrots have been and still are one of the most common and most widely distributed parrots of South America.

Aviculture: Red-vented parrots have been a more or less standard item in the pet trade only since the early 1970s. They are relatively suitable for an indoor cage even though many of them are very inactive there, sitting motionless on a perch for hours at a time without taking any notice of what is going on around them. They have so far exhibited little interest in or talent for talking. In aviaries, most red-vented parrots move about actively, become (or remain) quite tame, and start taking food from their caretaker's hand very soon.

Breeding: Sexing red-vented parrots is difficult. Sometimes the shape of the eye ring gives a clue. In the males it is generally round; in females, more oval.

The female initiates the courtship display by stalking up and down in front of the male with raised neck feathers and spread tail. At a later stage, she invites the male with soft chirpings to mount her.

At the Private Institute for Parrot Research in Oberhausen, where the first red-vented parrots in Germany hatched in 1982, the clutches have consisted of about four eggs. They are brooded for exactly 28 days by the female alone. In 1950, F. Hubbell of San Diego bred the first young in the United States, although the earliest recorded success was that of four young, which occurred in 1890 in the aviary of A. Maillard of Croisic, France. After a nestling period of approximately 10 weeks, the fully fledged young birds leave the nest. The youngsters have red or orange bands across the forehead, which clearly distinguish them from their parents and which give way after the juvenile molt to the typical blue head color of the species.

Maximilian's Parrot or Scaly-Headed Parrot:
Pionus maximiliani (Four Subspecies)

Description: Length: 11½ inches (29 cm). Male and female: Overall color, olive green; forehead and lores, dull black; throat, blue to violet; undertail coverts, red; underside of the tail, green with blue outer vanes; eyes, brown; bare eye rings, white, broken in places by bluish violet; bill, blackish but horn-colored at the tip of both the upper and lower mandibles; feet, grayish brown. Juveniles may have a red band on the forehead, which disappears after the juvenile molt.

Distribution: Eastern South America, from eastern and southwestern Brazil to northern Argentina.

Habitat: Open forests along riverbeds in savannas. With growing deforestation and the concomitant destruction of the birds' original biotopes, they are moving to different types of landscapes.

Aviculture: The birds that are sometimes offered quite cheaply at pet stores generally belong to the nominate form *P. m. maximiliani*; another subspecies, *P. m. siy*, which has a wider violet to blue throat band, is found only rarely.

Maximilian's parrots have similar requirements for care as red-vented and bronze-winged parrots. They become tame quickly and can develop into affectionate pets. We know nothing about their ability to mimic. Unfortunately, these birds quickly degenerate into impassive and lethargic creatures if they are confined to a cage. My own experience has shown that an aviary is the best kind of housing for Maximilian's parrots, but they have to have a large, heatable shelter where they can stay during prolonged spells of bad weather.

One peculiarity Maximilian's and occasionally red-vented parrots are given to is to let their heads droop down while sleeping or resting (the way hanging parakeets, *Loriculus*, do). The reason for this behavior is unclear.

Breeding: Very few Maximilian's parrots have been raised in aviaries so far. Probably the first success was scored by the Stoodleys of England (1975), followed in 1977 by two young, reared by H. Murray of Brentwood, Essex. The first parrots of this species to have been raised in Germany were born in 1977 and belonged to H. J. Geil of Meinhard. Incubation lasts 26 days, and the nestling period is about 60 days.

Bronze-winged Parrot:
Pionus chalcopterus (Two Subspecies)
Photograph on page 102.

Description: Length: 11 inches (28 cm). Male and female: head and underparts, bluish black; throat, creamy white; neck, pink; wing coverts, bronze-colored; flight feathers, dark blue; rump and underside of wings and tail, pale blue; undertail coverts, red; eyes, dark brown, surrounded by bare, pink eye rings; bill, yellowish; feet, flesh-colored. Juvenile birds have green wing coverts or green margins on them and yellowish eye rings.

Distribution: In northwestern South America, from northwestern Venezuela and northwestern Peru to western Ecuador and southwestern Colombia.

Habitat: Tropical and subtropical mountain forests.

Aviculture: Before 1970, this parrot was practically unknown among aviculturists and fanciers, but since then occasional advertisements for and reports about these birds have appeared. The bronze-winged parrot's coloring differs sharply from that of its close relatives, most of which are predominantly green, and at first glance, this bird looks rather sober and monochrome. Its full beauty becomes apparent only in a large outdoor aviary because the pale blue on the underside of the wings and tail together with the contrasting red near the vent are prominently displayed only in flight.

Numerous parrot owners have reported that bronze-winged parrots are very nervous in captivity and become highly agitated at the slightest disturbance. My own experience with five of these birds runs counter to this. My bronze-winged parrots took very little time getting used to their new living conditions and even accepted peanuts and pieces of fruit from my hand. I could detect no sign of nervousness in them. It is of course conceivable that birds removed from the wild at an older age have a harder time adjusting to the relative boredom of cage life than immature parrots.

Breeding: Thus far only a few of these parrots have reproduced in captivity. The first success was scored in 1974 by Swaenepoel of Belgium. Bronze-winged parrots were also raised by the Stoodleys of Hampshire, England, in 1973; by the Swiss aviculturist O. Meyer in 1980, and by W. Werner of the Federal Republic of Germany in 1983.

A clutch consists or a maximum of five eggs, which are incubated for 27–29 days. The nestling period is about 60 days.

Popular Parrot Species

Macaws

Macaws are divided into three — or according to some scientists, four — genera and are distributed over much of Central and South America. In earlier times they also inhabited some of the West Indies, but they became extinct there probably as early as the seventeenth century. Only the Cuban macaw survived as late as about 1880.

Of the macaws belonging to the *Anodorhynchus* genus, only the hyacinth macaw, the largest of all parrots, is occasionally imported into Europe and America. The two other species of this genus, Lear's and the glaucous macaw, are among the rarest birds of the world and are scarcely ever found in captivity. The same is true of the Spix macaw, the sole representative of the genus *Cyanopsitta*. Probably the only bird of this species accessible to public admiration lives in the bird park Walsrode in northern Germany.

The macaws a parrot fancier is likely to encounter all belong to the genus *Ara,* the true macaws. For many years now several *Ara* species have been more or less regularly imported. In addition to the familiar larger species, like the blue and gold, the green-winged, and the scarlet macaws, dwarf macaws have been imported in increasing numbers since the early 1970s. The noble macaw is the smallest of these. It is usually counted among the *Ara* genus, but because of external characteristics some scientists assign it to another genus, namely, *Diopsittica.*

Macaws require spacious quarters; keeping them permanently in cages does not agree with them. Aviaries have to consist of tough materials; ordinary wire grating will not stand up to their destructive bills for long. I recommend 4-m decorative spot-welded grating with a mesh size of 40–50 mm. If you do not have an aviary for your macaws, you can clip their wings and keep the birds on a climbing tree. The smaller macaw species can, if necessary, be kept in large cages or housed in medium-sized aviaries like those suitable for Amazons.

Most macaws are partially tamed before they are exported from their native countries. Even if they are not, most of them quickly become friendly. Some species are quite good mimics. The voices of all macaws are loud; some screech shrilly, and others emit monotonous calls several minutes long.

Large macaws have a tendency when living in domesticity to pluck their feathers, even if their quarters are on a generous scale. The reason for this is still insufficiently understood.

Blue and Gold Macaw: Ara ararauna

Photographs on pages 55, 56, and 119 and on back cover.

Description: Length: 34 inches (85 cm). Male and female: Upper parts, bright blue tinged with turquoise; underparts, bright, golden yellow; forehead and crown, green; ear coverts and sides of the neck, yellow; throat, blackish; wings and tail, blue; skin on cheeks, mostly bare but with a few rows of small, dark feathers; eyes, yellowish; bill, black; feet, gray.

Distribution: Almost all of northern South America, from Panama to northern Argentina; also Trinidad.

Popular Parrot Species

Habitat: Forests near rivers; swampy areas with palms. This species avoids the mountainous regions in western South America as well as the coastal regions in eastern Brazil.

Aviculture: The blue and gold macaw, also called the blue and yellow, is quite common among parrot fanciers. Its popularity derives largely from its gift for talking, which is often the reason that people buy it. Because of the species' huge area of distribution, it is apparently possible to catch the birds easily in many places, so that we see them relatively often in pet stores.

This macaw is totally unsuited for life in a parrot cage. The only way to accommodate a blue and gold macaw indoors would be to have a large climbing tree or a parrot stand for it. A bird this size generates so much dirt, noise, and smell that hardly anyone would want to have it inside.

I think the best idea is to have a pair of these macaws in a large aviary. The perches, nest boxes, and food dispensers have to be very solid and mounted securely to withstand assaults of the birds' powerful beaks. My blue and gold macaws accomplished the impressive feat of systematically hacking holes into the poured cement ceiling of their bird house until their labors were "slowed down" by the reinforcing grating buried in the cement.

Breeding: Apparently systematic efforts to breed blue and gold macaws have been underway for only a few years. Sexing these birds is relatively difficult; in addition to the general sex differences mentioned on page 53, the shade of yellow on the breast may give some clues; in males it is deep, almost orange-red, in females, paler yellow.

Large macaws rarely produce eggs before their sixth or seventh year, but they may earlier go through courtship displays and other behavior indicating sexual bonding.

A clutch usually contains two to three eggs, which are incubated by the female for about 25 days. The male guards the entry hole during this time or sits next to the female in the next box. After a nestling period of approximately 90 days, the fully fledged young birds emerge from the nest box. At this point they weight an average of 2.2–2.4 pounds (1000–1100 g).

Great Green Macaw:
Ara ambigua (Two Subspecies)
This species is in danger of becoming extinct and is therfore listed in Appendix I of the Washington Convention (see page 50).

Description: Length: 34 inches (85 cm). Male and female: Overall color, green; forehead, red; flight feathers, bluish green; undersides of wings and tail, yellowish olive; bare skin on the face, white to flesh-colored with five to six rows of small dark feathers under the eyes; eyes, yellow; bill, dark gray; feet, gray.

Popular Parrot Species

Distribution: *A. a. ambigua* is found in Nicaragua, Costa Rica, Panama, and western Colombia; *A. a. guayaquilensis,* in western Ecuador and possibly in southwestern Colombia.

Habitat: Forests in tropical and subtropical regions up to about 2000 feet (650 m) above sea level.

Military Macaw:
Ara militaris (Three Subspecies)
Photograph on page 119.

Description: Length: 28 inches (70 cm). Male and female: The military macaw resembles the great green macaw, but it has an olive brown spot on the throat. The plumage on the rump and back and near the vent is light blue, and the entire bird is considerably smaller.

Distribution: *A. m. militaris* occurs from northwestern Venezuela to eastern Ecuador and northern Peru; *A. m. mexicana,* throughout Mexico except in the rain forest zones; and *A. m. boliviana,* in the tropical zones of Bolivia and the northwesternmost tip of Argentina.

Habitat: Mostly dry forests and areas of open brush in arid zones up to about 8000 feet (2500 m).

Aviculture: The military and the great green macaws are sometimes mistaken for each other, although upon closer inspection the green color on the neck and back of the military is considerably darker than that of its relative. There is also a clear difference of size.

Military and great green macaws are less common in pet stores than other large macaws. However, the collections of almost every major zoo include great green macaws, usually in a mixed group together with blue and gold, green-winged, and scarlet macaws, whereas military macaws are much rarer in zoos and bird parks. In the fall of 1985, the great green macaw, including all subspecies, was added to Appendix I of the Washington Convention (see page 50).

Neither of these two species of macaws is encountered much in the aviaries of fanciers. Military macaws are said to make good indoor pet birds, assuming they have a sufficiently large cage or indoor aviary. If treated properly they become tame quickly and learn

Popular Parrot Species

to mimic human speech as well as other sounds. Like hyacinth macaws and some other large macaws, military macaws apparently are adept at learning tricks, such as roller skating or riding a bicycle — on special miniature models, of course — and thus often bring special applause at circus shows.

Keeping military macaws outdoors all day long is an option only in rural areas because of their ear-splitting utterances. If there are neighbors around, the birds should be left in their enclosed shelter during their vocal periods.

Breeding: In 1963, the first military macaw offspring in captivity were born in the Wellington Zoo in New Zealand, and the first great green macaw chicks hatched in the East Berlin Zoo in 1974. A clutch of either species consists of two to three eggs and is incubated for 25–27 days.

Scarlet Macaw:
Ara macao

Photographs on pages 38, 66, and 119 and on back cover.

This species, too, is in danger of extinction and is listed in Appendix I of the Washington Convention (see page 50).

Description: Length: 34 inches (85 cm). Male and female: Overall color, red; back, rump, upper tail coverts, and flight feathers, blue; wing coverts and scapulars, yellow; upper side of tail, scarlet with blue tips; underside of tail, brownish red; bare skin on the face, pink and — in some individuals — with a few rows of small, red feathers; eyes, yellow; upper mandible, horn-colored with black at the base; lower mandible, entirely black; feet, dark gray.

Distribution: Large sections of Central and South America. One population resides in Central America, from the state of Oaxaca in Mexico southward of southern Panama. A second population inhabits South America, east of the Andes, ranging from Colombia to Bolivia and eastward across Brazil to Guiana and the island of Trinidad.

Habitat: Forests near rivers in flatlands below 3300 feet (1000 m).

Aviculture: The scarlet macaw is one of the most familiar South American parrots. With its bright plumage, combining red, yellow, and blue in sharp contrast, it is one of the most brilliant parrots and for many people stands for what a parrot should look like. Together with the blue and gold and the green-winged macaws, it belongs to the standard offerings of just about any zoo or bird park. However, this bird is much less common among aviculturists. This is partly because the scarlet macaw requires unusually large and substantial quarters and has a harsh, piercing voice. This bird definitely does not belong in a cage. If you want a scarlet macaw and don't have an aviary, you can trim its flight feathers and let it live in a climbing tree or take it outdoors when it is warm enough.

Breeding: Although the scarlet macaw has never been imported in great numbers, this species has reproduced relatively well in captivity; the first time seems to have been early in the century in California. According to several reports, scarlet macaws become extremely aggressive during the mating season, resorting to loud screams and physical attack in the effort to drive away intruders — whether caretaker, visitor, dog, cat, or another parrot — that might pose a threat to the eggs or chicks.

The female lays two or three eggs and incubates them for about 26 days. It seems that the male may take an active part in incubating. The nestlings apparently develop more slowly than those of blue and gold or green-winged macaws. The nestling period is 90–100 days, and the average weight of the fledglings is between 23 and 28 ounces (650–800 g).

In captivity, scarlet macaws occasionally mate with blue and gold, green-winged, military, and hyacinth macaws and produce viable offspring.

Green-Winged Macaw:
Ara chloroptera
Photographs on page 19, 20, and 119 and on front and back covers.

Description: Length: 36 inches (90 cm). Male and female: Overall color, red, but somewhat darker than that of the scarlet macaw; median wing coverts and scapulars, green; back, rump, upper and undertail coverts, light blue; primaries, dark blue; tail, dark red with blue tips; underside of wings, reddish brown; bare skin on the face has some narrow rows of small, red feathers;

eyes, yellow; upper mandible, horn-colored and black at the base; lower mandible, entirely black; feet, dark gray.

Distribution: Large sections of South America, from Panama in the north to Paraguay and northern Argentina in the south, and from northwestern Colombia east of the Andes to Guiana and Venezuela.

Habitat: Primarily tropical forests in the lowlands and in foothills below 3300 feet (1000 m).

Aviculture: The green-winged macaw was first imported to Europe at the beginning of the seventeenth century. Today this parrot is found in all zoos and bird parks but not among many private owners. Perhaps most fanciers have second thoughts when they see the bird's impressive beak and hear its overpowering voice.

Like all other large macaws, the green-winged species becomes quite tame in captivity, although it does not have the same charm as the scarlet macaw.

Breeding: Because this bird is so often confused with its scarlet relative, it is impossible to state with absolute certainty when this species first reproduced in captivity.

Popular Parrot Species

Probably the first reliably identified green-winged macaw chicks were raised in 1962 by the English aviculturist J. S. Rigge. Others were raised in 1972 by the American H. J. Gregory of Lytle, Texas, and in 1977 by the Englishman N. Johnstone, Leicestershire. The Hannover Zoo, the bird park Metelen Heide, several other zoos, and some private parrot fanciers have also reported breeding successes.

Green-winged macaws usually lay two to three eggs, which the female incubates by herself for 27 days. At about 60 days, the young birds are fully fledged; however, the nestling period may last 90–100 days.

Green-winged macaws in captivity have somtimes mated with blue and gold or with scarlet macaws and have raised hybrid offspring successfully.

Yellow-Naped Macaw:
Ara auricollis
Photograph on page 120.

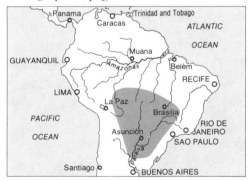

Description: Length: 15½ inches (38 cm). Male and female: Overall color, green; forehead, crown, throat, and lower cheeks, black-ish; collar on the nape, golden yellow; primaries and upper side of tail, bluish, interspersed with green and reddish brown; feet, flesh-colored; eyes, brownish red to orange; bare skin on the face, white; bill, dark, with a light tip on the upper mandible.

Distribution: Southern Brazil (Mato Grosso), much of Bolivia, northern Paraguay, and northwestern Argentina.

Habitat: Prefers subtopical forest areas close to watering places.

Aviculture: Before 1970, the yellow-naped macaw was considered a great rarity in the pet trade; then it began to be imported, at first occasionally and from about 1975–1980 quite regularly. Since then this influx has almost dried up again, and the birds have been imported only sporadically the last few years.

If my experience with a pair of these macaws is typical, yellow-naped macaws don't have as pleasant a disposition in captivity as their larger relatives. My birds, which are domestically raised juveniles that I took over from an acquaintance, acted much like the proverbial geese of the Roman Capitol. Just as the ancient geese warned the Romans with loud honking of the approach of an enemy, my yellow-naped macaws responded to the slightest activity near their aviary with ear-splitting screeching.

This constant noise went beyond what our generally understanding neighbors could endure, and I finally agreed to pass on the macaws. The decision was made all the easier because the birds refused to overcome their shyness and fluttered around wildly every time I entered the aviary.

Breeding: The first nonwild yellow-naped macaw chicks were hatched in 1976 in the

Popular Parrot Species

zoo of Bristol, England, and in the same year the bird park Walsrode in northern Germany also reported offspring. At Walsrode, close to thirty young yellow-naped macaws have been reared in the meantime. Two German aviculturists have also bred this macaw, namely, K. Maass in 1979 and H. Ploog in 1981. Maass found that in his pair the male had a considerably wider and deeper yellow collar than the female. A typical clutch consists of three or four eggs. They are incubated for about 28 days, and at 7 weeks the young are fully fledged. They leave the nest box at 9–10 weeks but are apparently not fully independent until 14–16 weeks of age.

Severe Macaw:
Ara severa (Two Subspecies)
See photograph on page 120.

Description: Length: 18 inches (45 cm). Male and female: Overall color, green; forehead and under the chin, dark brown; some feathers on crown, bluish green; bend of wing and speculum, red; distal vanes of primary coverts and flight feathers, rich blue; tail, brownish red above and purple below; bare facial area, whitish pink with several rows of tiny brown feathers; eyes, orange; bill, black; feet, grayish brown.

Distribution: Wide regions of South America, from Panama in the north to northern Bolivia and northwestern Brazil in the south and from western Colombia and Ecuador east of the Andes to the Orinoco region in Venezuela and to Guiana on the Atlantic.

Habitat: Mostly tropical forests, especially near rivers. Occasionally the birds forage for grain in cultivated areas.

Aviculture: Severe macaws look much like military macaws but are considerably smaller. For years these birds have been imported only sporadically.

All owners of these birds whom I know, as well as the literature I have been able to consult, agree that this macaw becomes tame quickly, especially when kept singly. Even if kept in pairs, however, severe macaws become quite attached to their keeper, although not completely tame.

The severe macaw's voice can be loud and harsh. One utterance sounds startlingly like the Latin genus name, *Ara.* Severe macaws are quite good mimics, and one fancier reports that his bird repeats not only words he has learned from people but also those voiced by an Amazon living in the same room.

Breeding: The San Diego Zoo of California reported the first domestic severe macaw chicks in 1940. Only two instances of these birds reproducing in Europe — apart from some hybrids and other doubtful cases — are known. O. Hirthe of Copenhagen reported success in 1954, and the Whipsnade Zoo in England in 1961.

The Danish aviculturist reports that his female bird laid and incubated three eggs, which after 26 days produced one chick. The nestling period was almost 8 weeks, and the young bird became independent at 14 weeks. Hirte's macaws produced offspring for several years in succession; in 1958, five eggs were laid, from which four chicks hatched and were reared.

The German parrot fancier M. K. Oehler of Friedrichshafen reported a set of hybrid chicks from the mating of a severe and an Illiger's macaw.

Illiger's Macaw:
Ara maracana

Description: Length: 17 inches (43 cm). Male and female: Overall color, green; forehead, red; head, nape, cheeks, and crown, bluish green; back and a V-shaped mark on the abdomen, red; flight feathers and primary coverts, blue; bend of wing, bluish green; upper side of the tail, blue with reddish brown toward the tip; eyes, orange-red; bare skin on the face, white; bill, black; feet, flesh-colored.

Distribution: Eastern Brazil south of the Amazon, Paraguay, and northeastern Argentina.

Habitat: Forests near the coast or near rivers. With increasing destruction of wilderness habitat, especially along the coast, Illiger's macaw has in recent years been forced to retreat more to the interior of the continent.

Aviculture: This bird is seldom offered for sale. When it is, it quickly finds buyers because of its reputation as a pleasant indoor pet and as a good mimic. Illiger's macaws also do well in an outdoor aviary, but they are sensitive to the cold.

Breeding: These birds have repeatedly been bred in captivity. Probably the first domestic offspring were born in 1931 at the London Zoo. Since then breeding successes have periodically been reported in avicultural publications.

One "prolific" pair of Illiger's macaws belongs to the German aviculturist F. Veser of Tettnang; his birds raised a total of fifty-three young between 1974 and 1982. The clutch always consisted of three to four eggs, which were incubated for about 26 days. The young generation of birds started laying fertilized eggs when only 2 years old.

The zoo of Duisburg in West Germany reported a set of Illiger's macaw chicks in 1979. There the incubation period was 24 days and the nestling period, 9 weeks. After leaving the nest, the young were fed by their parents for another 2 months. Unfortunately, the male parent died in 1982, and after a period of mourning the female, in the absence of a male of her own species, accepted a black-headed caique as her new partner. These two dissimilar birds proceeded to mate and, in 1984, raised four chicks that had the shape of their macaw mother and coloration that included characteristics of both parents. These two parent birds had produced fertilized eggs as early as 1983, but nobody had expected them to hatch because everyone assumed that two such dissimilar species could not possibly have viable offspring.

M. K. Oehler of Friedrichshafen, West Germany, had offspring from a crossing of a severe and an Illiger's macaw.

Noble Macaw or Red-Shouldered Macaw:
Ara nobilis (Three Subspecies)

Description: Length: 12 inches (30 cm). Male and female: Overall color, green; forehead and crown, bluish green; bend of wing and speculum, red; underside of tail and wings, olive yellow; eyes, reddish orange; bare skin on the face, white; bill, grayish black; feet, dark gray.

The subspecies *A. n. cumanensis* differs from the nominate form by its lighter bill.

Distribution: Extensive areas of South America, from Venezuela and Guinea in the northeast to southern Brazil.

Habitat: Tropical and subtropical forests as well as savannas.

Aviculture: Freshly imported birds are at first quite sensitive to the cold and should not be exposed to temperatures below 59°F (15°C) during their first winter. In the course of the second year they can be gradually introduced to the outdoors by having their cage moved to the garden or balcony for a few hours in good weather. Or, if they live in a birdhouse, the shutter to the outdoor flight can be opened for short periods. These birds should always have access to a nest box with thick walls, which they use for sleeping in all year.

For most parrots, keeping them in pairs is best, but noble macaws can also live together in a flock if there is enough room. They will even lay eggs and raise young in an aviary they share with others of their kind.

The volume and shrillness of the noble macaw's voice seems way out of proportion to the bird's modest size. Another "vice" this species is often given to in captivity is feather plucking, which even accommodating the birds in an outdoor aviary doesn't necessarily prevent. Some noble macaws pluck their feathers only at certain times of year.

Breeding: Apparently, the first noble macaws in captivity were born around 1940 in the United States. In Europe, the subspecies *A. n. cumanensis* first reproduced in England in 1949, and in the early 1970s the nominate race, too, produced offspring in England.

The first German aviculturist to breed noble macaws was W. de Grahl of Hamburg. Four eggs were laid in early March 1975, and in April one chick hatched. Its eyes opened after 18 days, and at the same time the first quills began to show through the skin. A

Popular Parrot Species

pletely fledged, and a few days later it emerged from the nest box.

Hyacinth Macaw:
Anodorhynchus hyacinthinus

Photograph on page 20.

This species is threatened with extinction and is listed in Appendix I of the Washington Convention (see page 138)!

Description: Length: 40 inches (100 cm). Male and female: Overall color, cobalt blue; underside of the tail, gray; the elastic skin at the base of the lower mandible and the bare eye ring are dark yellow; eyes, dark brown; bill, grayish black; feet, dark gray.

Distribution: Southern Brazil, especially the states of Para, Bahia, Goias, Minas Gerais, and Mato Grosso.

Habitat: Marshy forests and palm groves.

Aviculture: Hyacinth macaws have recently (1988) been added to the list of birds in Appendix I. Trade is no longer permitted, but hyacinth macaws are found more often than one might expect in private aviaries.

Providing adequate quarters for hyacinth macaws that not only satisfy the birds' need for exercise but also hold up under their destructive beaks runs into a fair amount of money. The aviary should be at least 12 × 18

feet (6 × 4 m) and 9 feet (3 m) high and be built of very substantial materials. In addition, there is the problem of noise. Most large macaws have loud, harsh voices, but hyacinth macaws seem to outdo them all. They produce their raucous calls at least twice a day, and even neighbors who are not very close and are basically fond of animals may find the racket unbearable. If a complaint about disturbance of the peace should reach the courts, the case would almost inevitably be decided against the parrot's owner.

Breeding: Trying to match a pair of hyacinth macaws is difficult because aviaries are seldom large enough for a small flock, and the birds can hardly ever be given a free choice of partners. Probably the first time hyacinth macaws were born in captivity was in 1968 at the zoo of Kobe, Japan; and in 1969 the zoo of Bratislava, Czechoslovakia, had a similar success. At the Chicago Zoo, hyacinth macaws were first hand-reared in 1971. The literature mentions only a few other instances of successful reproduction. A typical clutch consists of two or three eggs, from which the chicks hatch after about 30 days. There is no exact information on the length of the nesting period, but it seems to be between 90 and 100 days.

Caiques

Caique is the common name for parrots of the genus *Pionites*. This genus has only two species, the black-headed caique (*P. melano-cephala*) and the white-bellied caique (*P. leucogaster*). Two geographic subspecies or races are distinguished in the former, and three in the latter. Both species are apparently so closely related that some scientists

Popular Parrot Species

regard all caiques as a single species made up of five subspecies.

The characteristic feature of all caiques is the creamy white color of their breast plumage. Both species are occasionally imported. There are no external sex differences.

Acclimation is quite hard on caiques, and it is not uncommon for importers to lose birds during this adjustment period. Once caiques have come through the process, however, they are relatively resistant and can live to a considerable age in captivity. The literature mentions a black-headed caique that lived over 30 years.

The voices of caiques are shrill and penetrating, and if a flock of these birds is kept — which is quite feasible and sometimes done — their calls can be a serious nuisance for noise-sensitive neighbors.

Black-Headed Caique:
Pionites melanocephala (Two Subspecies)
Photograph on page 120.

Description: Length: 9 inches (23 cm). Male and female: Crown and forehead, black; lores, green; throat and neck, deep yellow; nape, brownish orange; back and wing and upper tail coverts, green; breast and abdomen, creamy white; thighs, flanks, and undertail coverts, yellowish orange; tail, gray with yellow tips above and olive yellow below; eyes, orange, surrounded by bare, gray eye rings; bill, black; feet, gray.

Distribution: North of the Amazon River, from Guiana on the Atlantic to eastern Ecuador in the west and northern Peru in the south.

Habitat: Forests and savannas in tropical lowlands; only occasionally at higher altitudes. This bird's native range has thus far been relatively untouched so that the species is still quite abundant over most of its area of distribution.

Aviculture: These parrots are available only sporadically because they are caught in much smaller numbers than Amazons. After a somewhat problematic acclimation period, black-headed caiques present no major problems, although they do have to be wintered over — like most South American parrots — in dry, draft-free, and heated shelters. Their nutritional requirements resemble those of other neotropical parrots (see page 35) but should be especially varied with plenty of fruit and occasional "lory meals" (canned fruit cocktail, diced fruits with corn syrup added to whole can of fruit, boiled rice with evaporated milk, and ABDEC multivitamin supplement).

One peculiarity worth mentioning is the black-headed caiques' play behavior. They express their high spirits by cavorting around the aviary and tussling with each other in a manner more reminiscent of kea parrots from faraway New Zealand than of their closer relatives. A small flock of black-headed caiques will live quite happily together in an aviary large enough for flying,

Popular Parrot Species

and apparently some birds have produced offspring under these conditions.

Breeding: It is impossible to determine the sex of black-headed caiques, and even their behavior gives no unequivocal clues. Males and females seem to behave exactly the same. In spite of this difficulty, a number of these birds have been successfully reared, especially in recent years. The last reported success I have seen was in 1983.

In the course of their courtship display, the male and the female approach each other with erect posture and bow several times to each other. Many birds incorporate nesting materials into their nest boxes, usually small twigs from which they remove the bark. Some females have also been observed lining their nests with feathers. A clutch consists of an average of three eggs, which the female sits on for about 26 days. The female feeds the nestlings entirely by herself for the first 9 days; then the male takes over some of the feeding. At about 55 days the young have acquired almost all their feathers, and they leave the nest box sometime between 60 and 75 days. They start feeding themselves without help from their parents at about 80-85 days.

White-Bellied Caique:
Pionites leucogaster (Three Subspecies) Photograph on page 120.

Description: Length: 9 inches (23 cm). Male and female: Forehead, crown, and nape, orange; lores, cheeks, and throat, olive yellow; breast and abdomen, creamy white; back, upper side of wings, underwing coverts, and upper tail coverts, green; flight feathers, bluish black; undertail coverts, yellow; *P. l. leucogaster* has green thighs, and in *P. l. xanthurus* and *P. l. xanthomeria* they

are yellow; eyes, red, with bare, pinkish gray eye rings; bill, horn-colored; feet, pink.

Distribution: South of the Amazon River from northern Bolivia, eastern Ecuador, and eastern Peru eastward to the Atlantic.

Habitat: Tropical forests, especially near moving water.

Aviculture: The white-bellied caique is imported much less frequently than its black-headed relative. Both species have similar requirements. They are so much alike in behavior that one ornithologist has suggested that the two caiques probably represent two races of the same species, especially since the only external difference between them is the color on the crown and forehead.

Breeding: Only a few white-bellied caiques have thus far been raised in captivity, all in the United States. A breeding attempt in England came to an abrupt end when three chicks that had been born were killed by their parents a few days after hatching. A "mixed marriage" between a black-headed and a white-bellied caique produced several offspring in an American zoo.

A clutch consists of three to four eggs, which are incubated from 26–30 days, and the young leave the nest after about 10 weeks.

Endangered and Extinct Species

Parrot Species in Danger of Extinction

Appendix I of the Washington Convention lists all the parrots that are in immediate danger of extinction or close to it. Trade in these birds is prohibited except for parrots that were raised in captivity. The most recent edition of Appendix I, drawn up at the fifth conference of May 1985, includes the following species.

Amazona versicolor, versicolor or St. Lucia Amazon
Amazona vinacea, vinaceous Amazon
Amazona vittata, Puerto Rican Amazon
Anadorhynchus glaucus, glaucous macaw (may be extinct)
Anadorhynchus hyacinthinus, hyacinth macaw
Anadorhynchus leari, Lear's macaw
Ara rubrogenys, red-fronted or red-crowned macaw
Ara glaucogularis, blue-throated macaw
Ara ambigua, great green macaw
Ara macao, scarlet macaw
Aratinga guarouba, golden conure
Cyanopsitta spixii, Spix's macaw
Cyanoramphus auriceps forbesi, subspecies of yellow-fronted parakeet
Cyanoramphus novaezelandiae, red-fronted parakeet
Opopsitta diophtalma coxeni, blue-browed or red-faced lorilet
Geopsittacus occidentalis, night parrot (may be extinct)
Neophema chrysogaster, orange-breasted parakeet
Pezoporus wallicus, ground parakeet
Pionopsitta pileata, red-capped or pileated parrot
Psephotus pulcherrimus, paradise parakeet (may be extinct)
Psittacula krameri echo, subspecies of Mauritius parakeet
Psittacula erithacus princeps, subspecies of gray parrot
Pyrrhura cruentata, red-eared conure
Rhynchopsitta spp., thick-billed parrots (two races)
Strigops habroptilus, owl parrot or kakapo
Amazona arausiaca, red-necked Amazon
Amazona barabdensis, yellow-shouldered Amazon
Amazona brasiliensis, red-tailed Amazon
Amazona guildingii, St. Vincent Amazon
Amazona imperialis, imperial Amazon
Amazona leucocophala, Cuban Amazon
Amazona pretrei, red-spectacled Amazon
Amazon dufresniana rhodocorytha, red-crowned Amazon

Extinct Species

A number of parrots became extinct during the eighteenth and nineteenth centuries. The reasons are not always known, but changes in and destruction of the parrots' natural habitat have been blamed as well as shooting of the birds for food and catching them for the pet trade. The following list contains all the species that are known to have existed, and in parentheses the date when they presumably died out is given.

Nestor meridionalis productus, Norfolk Island kaka (1851)
Charmosyna diadema, New Caledonian lorikeet (ca. 1860)
Cyanoramphus zealandicus, black-fronted parakeet (1844)
Cyanoramphus ulietanus, society parakeet (1773/4)
Cyanoramphus novaezelandiae subflavescens, subspecies of red-fronted parakeet (ca. 1870)
Cyanoramphus novaezelandiae erythrotis, subspecies of red-fronted parakeet (1800 to 1820)
Mascarinus mascarinus, Mascarene parrot (1800–1820)
Psittacula eupatria wardi, Seychelles parakeet (ca. 1870)
Psittacula exsul, Newton's parakeet (ca. 1875)
Loriculus philippensis chrysonotus, subspecies of Philippine hanging parrot (after 1926)
Amazona vittata gracilipes, subspecies of Puerto Rican Amazon (1899)
Aratinga chloroptera maugei, Mauge's conure (ca. 1860)
Conuropsis carolinensis carolinensis, Carolina parakeet (ca. 1900)
Conuropsis carolinensis ludovicianus, subspecies of the above (1914)
Ara tricolor, Cuban macaw (1885)

Special Rules for Bringing Pet Birds into the United States

What Is a Pet Bird?

A pet bird is defined as any bird, except poultry, intended for the personal pleasure of its individual owner, not for resale. Poultry, even if kept as pets, are imported under separate rules and quarantined at USDA animal import centers. Birds classified as poultry include chickens, turkeys, pheasants, partridge, ducks, geese, swans, doves, peafowl, and similar avian species.

Importing a Pet Bird

Special rules for bringing a pet bird into the United States (from all countries but Canada):

* USDA quarantine
* Quarantine space reservation
* Fee in advance
* Foreign health certificate
* Final shipping arrangements
* Two-bird limit

If you're bringing your pet bird into the country, you must:

Quarantine your bird (or birds) for at least 30 days in a USDA-operated import facility at one of nine ports of entry. The bird, which must be caged when you bring it in, will be transferred to a special isolation cage at the import facility.

Reserve quarantine space for the bird. A bird without a reservation will be accepted only if space is available. If none exists, this bird either will be refused entry or be transported, at your expense, to another entry port where there is space.

Pay the USDA an advance fee of $40 to be applied to the cost of quarantine services and necessary tests and examinations. Currently, quarantine costs are expected to average $80 for one bird or $100 per isolation cage if more than one bird is put in a cage. These charges may change without notice. You may also have to pay private companies for brokerage and transportation services to move the bird from the port of entry to the USDA import facility.

Obtain a health certificate in the nation of the bird's origin. This is a certificate signed by a *national government* veterinarian stating that the bird has been examined, shows no evidence of communicable disease, and is being exported in accordance with the laws of that country. The certificate must be signed within 30 days of the time the birds arrive in the United States. If not in English, it must be translated at your cost.

Arrange for shipping the bird to its final destination when it is released from quarantine. A list of brokers for each of the nine ports of entry may be requested from USDA port veterinarians at the time quarantine space is reserved. (See addresses to follow.) Most brokers offer transportation services from entry port to final destination.

Bring no more than two psittacine birds (parrots, parakeets, and other hookbills) per family into the United States during any single year. Larger groups of these birds are imported under separate rules for commercial shipment of birds. Rules effective January 15, 1980.

(Reprinted with permission from USDA-APHIS.)

Ports of Entry for Personally Owned Pet Birds

Listed below are the nine ports of entry for personally owned pet birds. To reserve quarantine space for your bird, write to the port veterinarian at the city where you'll be arriving and request Form 17-23. Return the completed form, together with a check or money order (contact the veterinarian in charge of the import facility for current costs) made payable to the USDA, to the same address. The balance of the fee will be due before the bird is released from quarantine.

Port Veterinarian
Animal and Plant Health Inspection Service (APHIS)
U.S. Department of Agriculture
(City, State, Zip Code)
New York, New York 11430
Miami, Florida 33152
Laredo, Texas 78040
El Paso, Texas 79902
Nogales, Arizona 85621
San Ysidro, California 92073
Los Angeles, California (Mailing address, Lawndale, CA 90261)
Honolulu, Hawaii 96850

The Quarantine Period

During quarantine, pet birds will be kept in individually controlled isolation cages to prevent any infection from spreading. Psittacine or hookbilled birds will be identified with a leg band. They will be fed a medicated feed as required by the U.S. Public Health Service to prevent psittacosis, a flulike disease transmissible to humans. Food and water will be readily available to the birds. Young, immature birds needing daily hand-feeding cannot be accepted because removing them from the isolation cage for feeding would interrupt the 30-day

Special Rules for Bringing Pet Birds into the United States

quarantine. During the quarantine, APHIS veterinarians will test the birds to make certain they are free of any communicable disease of poultry. Infected birds will be refused entry; at the owner's option they will either be returned to the country of origin (at the owner's expense) or humanely destroyed.

Special Exceptions

No government quarantine (and therefore no advance reservations or fees) and no foreign health certificate are required for:

• *U.S. birds taken out of the country if special arrangements are made in advance.* Before leaving the United States, you must get a health certificate for the bird from a veterinarian accredited by the USDA and make certain it is identified with a tattoo or numbered leg band. The health certificate, with this identification on it, must be presented at the time of re-entry. While out of the country, you must keep your pet bird separate from other birds. Remember that only two psittacine or hookbilled birds per family per year may enter the United States. Birds returning to the United States may come in through any one of the nine ports of entry listed earlier. There are also certain other specified ports of entry for these birds, depending upon the time of arrival and other factors. Contact APHIS officials for information on this prior to leaving the country.

• *Birds from Canada.* Pet birds may enter the United States from Canada on your signed statement that they have been in your possession for at least 90 days, were kept separate from other birds during the period, and are healthy. As with other countries, only two psittacine birds per family per year may enter the United States from Canada. Birds must be inspected by an APHIS veterinarian at designated ports of entry for land, air, and ocean shipments. These ports are subject to change, so for current information, contact APHIS/USDA officials.

Pet birds from Canada are not quarantined because Canada's animal disease control and eradication programs and import rules are similar to those of the United States.

Other U.S. Agencies Involved with Bird Imports

In addition to the U.S. Public Health Service requirement mentioned earlier, U.S. Department of the Interior rules require an inspection by one of its officials to assure that an imported bird is not in the rare or endangered species category, is not an illegally imported migratory bird, and is not an agricultural pest or injurious to humans. For details from these agencies, contact:

Division of Law Enforcement,
Fish and Wildlife Service,
U.S. Department of the Interior,
Washington, D.C. 20240

Bureau of Epidemiology,
Quarantine Division,
Center for Disease Control,
U.S. Public Health Service,
Atlanta, Georgia 30333

U.S. Customs Service,
Department of the Treasury,
Washington, D.C. 20229

For additional information on USDA-APHIS regulations, contact,

Import-Export Staff,
Veterinary Services, APHIS,
U.S. Department of Agriculture,
Hyattsville, Maryland 20782.

Two Serious Threats to Birds

As a bird owner, you should know the symptoms of exotic *Newcastle disease,* the devastating disease of poultry and other birds mentioned elsewhere. If your birds show signs of incoordination and breathing difficulties — or if there should be any unusual die-off among them — contact your local veterinarian or animal health official immediately. Place dead birds in plastic bags, and refrigerate them for submittal to a diagnostic laboratory. Keep in mind that this disease is highly contagious, and you should isolate any newly purchased birds for at least 30 days. Although exotic Newcastle disease is not a general health hazard, it can cause minor eye infection in humans.

If you're tempted to buy a bird you suspect may have been smuggled into the United States, don't! Smuggled birds are a persistent threat to the health of pet birds and poultry flocks in this country. Indications are that many recent outbreaks of exotic Newcastle disease were caused by birds entering the United States illegally. If you have information about the possibility of smuggled birds, report it to any U.S. Customs office or call APHIS at Hyattsville, Maryland, (301) 436-8061.

Issued January 1980.
Slightly revised November 1980.

Useful Literature and Addresses

Books

Cayley, N. W., and Lendon, A. (1973). *Australian Parrots in Field and Aviary*, Angus & Robertson, Sydney, Australia.

Deimer, P. (1983). *Parrots*, Barron's Educational Series, Woodbury, New York.

Eastman, W. R., and Hunt, A. C. (1966). *The Parrots of Australia*, Angus & Robertson, Sydney, Australia.

Forshaw, J. M. (1981). *Australian Parrots*, 2nd edition, Lansdowne Press, Melbourne, Australia.

———— (1978). *Parrots of the World*, 2nd edition, Lansdowne Press, Melbourne, Australia.

Harman, I. (1981). *Australian Parrots in Bush and Aviary*, Inkata Press, Melbourne and Sydney, Australia.

Low, R. (1980). *Parrots, Their Care and Breeding*, Blandford Press, Poole, Dorset, England.

———— (1984). *Endangered Parrots*, Blandford Press, Poole, Dorset, England.

Petrak, M. L. (1982). *Diseases of Cage and Aviary Birds*, 2nd edition, Lea & Febiger, Philadelphia.

Ruthers, A., and Norris, K. A. (1972). *Encyclopedia of Aviculture*, Vol. 2, Blandford Press, Poole, Dorset, England.

Vriends, M. M. (1986). *Lovebirds*, Barron's Educational Series, Woodbury, New York.

———— (1986). *Simon & Schuster's Guide to Pet Birds*, Simon & Schuster, New York.

———— (1985). *The Macdonald Encyclopedia of Cage and Aviary Birds*, Macdonald & Co., Publishers, Ltd., London and Sydney, Australia.

———— (1984). *Popular Parrots*, 2nd edition, Howell Book House, Inc., New York.

Periodicals

American Cage Bird Magazine (Monthly; One Glamore Court, Smithtown, New York, 11787)

Avicultural Bulletin (Monthly; Avicultural Society of America, Inc., P. O. Box 2796, Dept. CB, Redondo Beach, CA 90278)

Avicultural Magazine (Quarterly; The Avicultural Society, Windsor, Forest Stud, Mill Ride, Ascot, Berkshire, England)

Cage and Aviary Birds (Weekly; Prospect House, 9-15 Ewell Road, Cheam, Sutton, Surrey, SM3 8BZ, England); young birdkeepers under 16 may like to join the *Junior Bird League*; full details can be obtained from the J.B.L., c/o *Cage and Aviary Birds*

Magazine of the Parrot Society (Monthly; 19a De Parys Ave., Bedford, Bedfordshire, England)

Parrotworld (Monthly; National Parrot Association, 8 North Hoffman Lane, Hauppauge, New York, 11788)

Watchbird (Bi-monthly; American Federation of Aviculture, P. O. Box 1568, Redondo Beach, CA 90278)

American Bird Clubs

Avicultural Society of America (see *Avicultural Bulletin*)
American Federation of Aviculture, Inc. (see *The A.F.A. Watchbird*)
National Parrot Association (see *Parrotworld*)

Australian Bird Clubs

Avicultural Society of Australia, c/o Mr. I. C. L. Jackson, Box 130, Broadford, Victoria, 3658
Avicultural Society of Queensland, 19 Fahey's Road, Albany Creek, Queensland, 4035

Canadian Bird Clubs

Avicultural Advancement Council, P. O. Box 5126, Postal Station "B", Victoria, British Columbia, V8R 6N4
British Columbia Avicultural Society, c/o Mr. Paul Prior, 11784-90th Avenue, North Delta, British Columbia, V4C 3H6
Calgary and District Avicultural Society, c/o Mr. Richard Kary, 7728 Bowcliffe Cr., N.W., Calgary, Alberta, T3B 2S5
Canadian Parrot Association, Pine Oaks, R.R. Nr. 3, St. Catharines, Ontario, L2R 6P9

English Bird Clubs

The Avicultural Society (see *Avicultural Magazine*)
The Parrot Society (see *Magazine of the Parrot Society*)

New Zealand Bird Club

The Avicultural Society of New Zealand Inc., P. O. Box 21403, Henderson, Auckland 8

Veterinarian Association

Association of Avian Veterinarians, P. O. Box 299, East Northport, New York, 11731

Index

Note: Page numbers referring to illustrations are in *italics*.

Age
  at purchase, 13
  determination of, 58–59
Amazon
  blue-fronted, *65*, 115–117
  Finsch's, 114
  green-cheeked, 113
  mealy, 121–122
  orange-winged, 118, 121
  sexing of, 57
  species, 111
  spectacled, *6, 102*, 112
  yellow-cheeked, *66, 102*, 114–115
  yellow-fronted, *91*, 117–118
  yellow-naped, 37
Amazona
  aestiva, 115–117
  albifrons, 112
  amazonica, 118, 121
  autumnalis, 114–115
  farinosa, 121–122
  finschi, 114
  ochrocephala, 117–118
  viridigenalis, 113
Anatomy, *49*
Animal proteins, 40
Anodorhynchus hyacinthinus, 135
Ara
  ambigua, 127–128
  auricollis, 131–132
  chloroptera, 130–131
  macao, 129–130
  maracana, 133–134
  militaris, 128–129
  nobilis, 134
  severa, 132–133
  ararauna, 126–127
Artificial incubation, 76
Artificial light, 23
Aspergillosis, 45–46
Australian rose-breasted cockatoo, *83–84*
Aviary
  adjustment to, 26
  cleaning of, 31
  indoor, 16–17, *17*
  indoor-outdoor, 21
  outdoor, 22–23
Aviary birds, 25–26

Aviary room, 18, 21
Aviculturist, role of, 51–52
Avitaminosis-B6, 47

Bare-eyed cockatoo, *74, 84*, 100, 103
Bathing, 90
Bathing dish, 24, *25*
Beak
  care of, 90
  malformations of, 13
  opening of, 93
  shapes of, *20*
  trimming of, 32
Begging posture, 71
Behavior, 26–27, *56*
  courtship, 70–71, *70–71*
  mating, 71–72, *72*
  nonsocial, 88–91
  social, 91–94
Bird room 17–18
Birdseed, basic mixture, 35
Bird shows, 78–80
Black-headed caique, *120*, 136–137
Blue and gold macaw, *55, 94, 119*, 126–127
Blue-fronted Amazon, *65*, 115–117
Body parts, names of, *49*
Bottom tray, 15
Branches, 15, 40
Breeder birds, 52–53, 60–61
Breeding
  aviculturist's role in, 51–52
  courtship ritual, 70–71, *70–71*
  egg laying, incubation and hatching, 72–74
  extinction, threat of, 50
  housing of breeder birds, 52–53
  incubation period, 69
  matching pairs, 62–63
  mating, 71–72, *72*
  molting cycle and temperature, 63–64
  nesting, 64, 67–68
  purchase of breeder birds, 59–61
  sexing birds, 53–54, 57–58
  sexual maturity and age determination, 58–59
  single birds, mating of, 61–62
  supplementary foods for, 68–69
  Washington Convention, 50–51
  See also Bird shows; Development

Bronze-winged parrot, *102*, 125
Brown parrot, *101*, 108
Building permit, 21
Burglar alarm systems, 21–22
Cacatua
  alba, 98–99
  galerits, 95–96
  goffini, 99–100
  moluccensis, 97–98
  sanguinea, 100, 103
  sulphurea, 96–97
Cage door, 15
Cages
  accessories for, 15–16
  cleaning of, 31
  indoor, 14, *15*
Caique
  black-headed, *120*, 136–137
  sexing of, 57
  species, 135–136
  white-bellied, *120*, 137
Calcium supplements, 40
Captivity-reared birds, 11–12
Care, basic rules of
  acclimating aviary birds, 25–26
  catching a bird, 31
  cleaning of cage or aviary, 31
  dangers, list of, 34
  flying free, 29
  grooming requirements, 31–33, *32*
  mimicry, training for, 29–30
  settling in, 25
  toys, 30–31
  trip home, 25
Catching a bird, 31
Chains, 23
Characteristics of parrots, 81
Chicks, *66*
Children, 8
Climbing tree, 23, *23*
Clutch, 72
Coccidiosis, 44
Cockatoo
  Australian rose-breasted, *83–84*
  bare-eyed, *74, 84*, 100, 103
  Goffin's, *20*, 99–100
  greater sulfur-crested, *28*, 95–96
  lesser sulfur-crested, *9*, 96–97
  Moluccan, 97–98
  rose-breasted, *62, 66*, 103–104
  umbrella-crested, *25*, 98–99

Index

Coloration, 81
Comfort behavior, 89–91
Courtship ritual, 70–71, *70–71*
Crop inflammation, 45
Crop milk, 74, 92
Cuttlebone, 40

Development, 74–75, *75*
Diet
  animal proteins, 40
  basic birdseed mixture, 35
  of breeding birds, 68–69
  buying and storing birdseed, 36
  drinking water, 41
  feeding rules, 39
  fruits and vegetables, 36, 39
  minerals and vitamins, 40–41
  sprouted seeds, 39–40
Dimmer, 23
Diseases
  aspergillosis, 45–46
  avitaminosis-B6 (vitamin B
    deficiency), 47
  coccidiosis, 44
  crop inflammation, 45
  ectoparasites, 43
  egg binding, 48
  endoparasites, 43
  feather plucking, 47–48
  illness, first signs of, 42
  intestinal infections, 43–44
  parrot fever (Psittacosis), 46
  respiratory system disorders, 45
  rickets, 47
  salmonellosis, 44
  trichomoniasis, 44
Dishes, *See* Bathing; Food; Water
  dishes
Drinking habits, 89
Drinking water, 41
Droppings, 13

Eclectus parrots, *51, 101*, 105–106
  sexing of, 54
Eclectus roratus, 105–106
Ectoparasites, 43
Egg binding, 48
Eggs
  artificial incubation of, 76
  hatching of, 73–74
  laying of, 72
Egg yolk, hard-boiled, 40, 68

Enclosed shelter, 21–22
Endangered species, 138
Endoparasites, 43
Endoscopy, 58
Enteritis, 43
Eolophus roseicapillus, 103–104
Extinct species, 138
Eyes, 81–82

Feather plucking, 13, *19*, 47–48
Feeding (of chicks), 74, *74*
Feeding, rules for, 39
Feet, 81
Finsch's Amazon, 114
Flying capacity, 26, 88
Flying free (in apartment), 29
Food. *See* Diet
Food dishes, 15–16, *16*, 24
Food intake, 88–89
Food preference, 35
Foot boxing, 93
Foot care, 90
Foot raising, 93
Foundation (outdoor aviary), 22
Fruits, 36, 39

Goffin's cockatoo, *20*, 99–100
Grating
  for indoor aviary, 17
  for indoor cage, 14–15
Gray parrot, *10, 20, 66, 93*, 109–111
  sexing of, 57
Greater sulfur-crested cockatoo,
  28, 95–96
Great green macaw, 127–128
Green-cheeked Amazon, 113
Greens, 36
Green-winged macaw, *19, 119*, 130–
  131
Grit, 15, 40
Grooming
  clipping the wings, 32–33, *33*
  showers, 31–32
  trimming of toenails and beak,
    32, *32*

Habitat, natural, 85
Hairworms (*Capillaria*), 43
Hand-raised nestlings, feeding of,
  76–77
Hand-taming, 27
Hatching, 73
Health certificate, 139

Hearing, sense of, 82
Heating requirements, 23
Heterosexuality, checking for, 62
Housing
  aviary room, 18, 21
  bird room, 17
  of breeder birds, 52–53
  cage accessories, 15–16, 17
  enclosed shelter, 21–22
  indoor aviary, 16–17
  indoor cages, 14
  indoor-outdoor aviary, 21
  lighting and heating require-
    ments, 23
  outdoor aviary, 22–23
  temperature requirements, 24
Hyacinth macaw, *20*, 135
Hybrid offspring, 77–78

Illiger's macaw, 133–134
Illness, first signs of, 42. *See also*
  Diseases
Importing birds
  ports of entry for, 139
  special exceptions, 140
  special rules for, 139
  U.S. agencies involved with, 140
Imprinting, 61
Incubation period, 69, 73
Indoor aviary, 16–17, *17*
Indoor-outdoor aviary, 21
Infrared lamp, 42, *42*
Intestinal infections, 43–44

Jardine's parrot, *13*, 108–109
Juvenile birds, age determination of,
  58–59

Lesser sulfur-crested cockatoo, 9, 96–97
Lice, 43
Lighting requirements, 23
Litter, 16
Locomotion, 88
Long-winged parrots, 106–109
Macaw
  blue and gold, *55, 94, 119*, 126–127
  great green, 127–128
  green-winged, *19, 20, 119*, 130–131
  hyacinth, *20*, 135
  Illiger's, 133–134
  military, *119*, 128–129
  noble, 134
  scarlet, *38, 66, 94, 119*, 129–130

Index

severe, *120*, 132–133
sexing of, 57
species, 126
yellow-naped, *120*, 131–132
Matching pairs, 62–63, *62*
Mating, 71–72, *72*
Mating bond, 92
Maximilian's parrot, 124
Mealy Amazon, 121–122
Military macaw, *119*, 128–129
Mimicry, ability for, 29–30
Minerals, 40
Mites, 43
Molting cycle, effect of temperature on, 63–64
Moluccan cockatoo, 97–98
Mutual preening, 70, 92

Natural light, 23
Nesting
  bedding for, 68
  in wild, 86
  nest boxes, 64, 67, *68*
Nestling period, 75
Newcastle disease, 140
Noble macaw, 134
Nonsocial behavior, 88–91
Nourishment, state of, 13

Orange-winged Amazon, 118, 121
Outdoor aviary, 22–23

Paired birds, 7
Parrot fever (Psittacosis), 46
Parrot relatives, 81
Partner feeding, 70, 71, 92
Pecking fights, 94, *94*
Perches, 15
Pet bird, 139
Pioniles
  leucogaster, 137
  melanocephala, 136–137
Plumage, 12–13, *49*
Poicephalus
  African, 17
  gulielmi, 108–109
  meyeri, 108
  senegalus, 106–107
  sexing of, 54, 57
Pionus
  chalcopterus, 125
  menstruus, 123–124
  sexing of, 57

species, 122–123
  Maximilliani, 124
Preening, *10, 28, 30, 55*, 70, 89
Private owners, buying from, 11
Psittacosis, 46
Psittacus erithacus, 109–111
Psychic disturbances, 13
Punishment, 29
Purchase
  age of bird, 13
  signs to watch for, 12–13
  sources for, 11–12

Quarantine period, 25, 140

Raising parrots. *See* Breeding
Rearing food, 68–69, 76–77
Red-sided eclectus parrot, *101*
Red-vented parrot, *102*, 123–124
Respiratory disorders, 45, *45*
Resting and sleeping, 91, *92*
Rickets, 47
Roof (outdoor aviary), 23
Rose-breasted cockatoo, *62, 66*, 103–104
Roundworms (*Ascaridia*), 43

Salmonellosis (Paratyphoid infection), 44
Sand, 40
Scarlet macaw, *38, 66, 94, 119*, 129–130
Scientific classification, 81
Scratching, 89
Seed shelling, *89*
Senegal parrot, *101*, 106–107
Sensory organs, 81–82
Serious battles, 94
Several birds, 7–8
Severe macaw, *120*, 132–133
Sexing birds, 53–54, 57–58, *57*
Sexual maturity, 58
Shaking, 89
Shipping through mail, 11
Showers, 31–32, 90
Shyness, 26–27
Single birds, 7
  adjustment of, 26–27
  mating of, 61–62
Size
  of aviaries, 17
  of aviary room, 18
  of cages, 14

of eggs, 72
of nesting box, 67
of outdoor aviary, 22
Smuggled birds, 140
Social behavior, 91–94, *93–94*
Spectacled Amazon, *6, 102*, 112
Sprouted seeds, 39–40
Stool sample, 25–26, 42
Stretching, 90
Sunflower seeds, 35, 36, 39, 40

Taming, 27–29
Tapeworms (*Cestoda*), 43
Taste, sense of, 82
Temperature requirements, 24
Threatening stance, *79*, 93, *93*
Timer, 23
Toe arrangement, 81
Toenails, trimming of, 32, *32*
Toys, 16, 30–31
Transport box, 25, *26*
Trichomoniasis, 44
Trip home, 25

Umbrella-crested cockatoo, *25*, 98–99

Vacation care, 8
Vegetables, 36, 39
Vitamin B deficiency, 47
Vitamins, 41

Walls (aviary), 18
Warning and attack behavior, 92–93
Washington Convention (CITES), 50–51
Water dishes, 15, 24
White-bellied caique, *120*, 137
Wild fruits, 36, 39
Wild parrots
  incubation and rearing of young, 86–87
  nesting places, 86
Wild plants, 36, 39
Wing clipping, 26, 32–33, *33*
Wood shavings, 68

Yawning, 91, *91*
Yellow-cheeked Amazon, *66, 102*, 114–115
Yellow-fronted Amazon, *91*, 117–118
Yellow-naped Amazon, *37*
Yellow-naped macaw, *120*, 131–132
Yoghurt, 40